PUB WAL
FOR THE FA

Hampshir
AND THE NEW FOREST

PUB WALKS
FOR THE FAMILY

Hampshire
AND THE NEW FOREST

Nick Channer

COUNTRYSIDE BOOKS
NEWBURY, BERKSHIRE

Publisher's Note

We hope that you obtain considerable enjoyment from this book; great care has been taken in its preparation. However, changes of landlord and actual closures are sadly not uncommon. Likewise, although at the time of publication all routes followed public rights of way or permitted paths, diversion orders can be made and permissions withdrawn.

We cannot of course be held responsible for such diversion orders and any resultant inaccuracies in the text which result from these or any other changes to the routes nor any damage which might result from walkers trespassing on private property. We are anxious that all details covering the walks and the pubs are kept up to date and would therefore welcome information from readers which would be relevant to future editions.

First Published 1994
© Nick Channer 1994

All rights reserved. No reproduction
permitted without the prior permission
of the publishers:

COUNTRYSIDE BOOKS
3 Catherine Road
Newbury, Berkshire

ISBN 1 85306 317 7

Designed by Mon Mohan
Cover illustration by Colin Doggett
Photographs by the author
Maps by Bob Carr

Produced through MRM Associates Ltd., Reading
Typeset by Paragon Typesetters, Clwyd
Printed in England

Contents

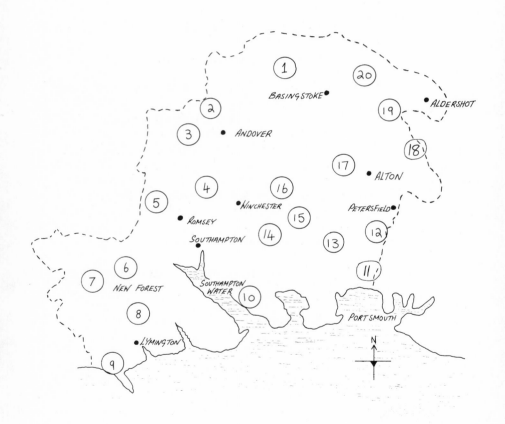

Area map showing locations of the walks.

Introduction

It has often been said that the county of Hampshire has something for everyone. With its scenic coastline, charming villages, rolling farmland and spectacular forests and woodland, its attractions are certainly many and varied. Much of it conveys a sense of space and quiet beauty in a shrinking world.

The countryside of mid and north Hampshire is still surprisingly unspoilt. In these parts of the county you can escape the pressures of modern life and enter a world of green fields, hidden valleys and wide, windswept landscapes, where you might not meet another soul. Even some of the villages are a reminder of how England used to be.

The river valleys and watermeadows of mid and south Hampshire are some of the finest in the country – the sparkling waters of the Itchen, Meon and Test adding an extra touch of beauty to their surroundings. Much of Hampshire is heavily wooded, especially the New Forest, which lies in the south-west corner of the county. Stretching for 20 miles and established as a deer park by William the Conqueror, the Forest is the jewel in Hampshire's crown. However, there are other lesser-known forests and extensive areas of woodland within Hampshire's boundaries. The wooded remnants of the ancient Forest of Bere can still be seen, while the Alice Holt Forest and the Queen Elizabeth Country Park are popular amenity areas with many attractions for walkers and cyclists.

Hampshire's coast is both spectacular and historic. The views over Southampton Water, the Isle of Wight and the Solent are a constant reminder of Britain's seafaring traditions.

The walks in this book are aimed at all age groups and are intended to take advantage of Hampshire's glorious scenery and attractions. There are entertaining and informative places of interest along the way which will appeal to both children and adults. For example, you can visit a famous zoological park, historic abbey, an isolated castle overlooking the Solent and a wildlife conservation centre – among other sites of interest which will enable you to spend an enjoyable day in the countryside.

Each walk is circular and starts and finishes at an inn where families are welcome and food is served. Many of the pubs I have chosen have a family room. Several have really excellent facilities for children, including indoor games and a safe, well-equipped play area in the garden. Some also have a special junior menu. Times of opening and other details are included. The walks are fairly short and, on the whole, quite easy. Those who are relatively inexperienced when it comes to a country ramble should not find these routes particularly difficult or demanding. It is advisable to take a copy of the relevant Ordnance Survey map with you, as well as some form of basic waterproof clothing – just in case the weather changes suddenly. It is also worth remembering that, whilst many of these routes will be bone dry in summer, in the winter months they can, in places, become extremely wet and muddy underfoot. The New Forest is a good example of how woodland rides and paths can become sodden with rain. A good pair of walking shoes or boots is therefore essential.

Permission has been given for cars to be left at the inns whilst the walks are undertaken, but it is advisable to check with the landlord before setting out.

Taking a stroll in Britain's rural heartland is really the only way to fully appreciate the natural state of our countryside. You can see and learn so much more on foot than you would from a speeding car. To add to the enjoyment of a day I always think it is important to seek out a traditional country inn where you will be suitably fed and watered. I hope the pubs and the walks in this book ensure that your day out in the Hampshire air is a pleasurable one.

Nick Channer
summer 1994

1 Ecchinswell
The Royal Oak

The Royal Oak was built as an inn and dates back to the 18th century. Families are made very welcome and can be accommodated in the spacious lounge bar and dining area at the rear of the pub. There is a large garden, also at the back – among the attractions are swings and various traditional pub games, including petanque. There are good views of the adjoining village stream with its assortment of ducks.

Inside, prints of animal and country scenes adorn the walls, and a popular games room is at the front of the inn. Home-made dishes are available every day and include chicken Kiev, chicken in breadcrumbs, lasagne, chilli with rice, steak and mushroom pie, stuffed boneless plaice, scampi, cottage pie, rump steak and T-bone steak. For something lighter you could opt for soup and sandwiches or ploughman's. The choice of puddings includes apple pie, jam or syrup roly-poly and cheesecake. There is also a traditional Sunday roast. London Pride, Wadworth 6X and Morland Speckled Hen are among the

9

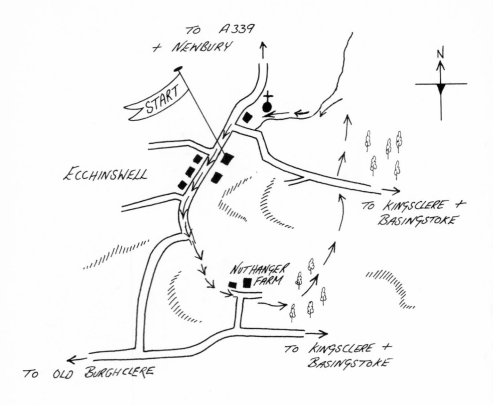

real ales, and Scrumpy Jack draught cider, Murphy's Irish Stout, Carling Black Label and Tennents Extra, are also on offer.

The times of opening are 12 noon to 4 pm and 6 pm to 11 pm on weekdays, all day on Saturday, and 12 noon to 3 pm and 7 pm to 10.30 pm on Sunday.

Telephone: 0635 298280.

How to get there: From the A339 Newbury to Basingstoke road, the turning to Ecchinswell is just to the south of the old Greenham Common airfield. The Royal Oak is in the village centre.

Parking: There is a car park at the inn. Some alternative parking spaces are available in the village.

10

Length of the walk: 2 ¾ miles. Map: OS Landranger 174 Newbury and Wantage (inn GR 498595)

The isolated countryside to the north of Hampshire has changed little over the years. There is a timeless quality to it and some of the villages, too, have an air of the past about them. This walk unearths some memorable views of the North Hampshire hills and in particular the peaceful slopes of Watership Down. It even passes Nuthanger Farm which features in Richard Adams' enchanting tale of rabbit folk. The final leg of the walk is beside an idyllic, tree-shaded stream near Ecchinswell church.

The Walk

On leaving the Royal Oak, turn left and walk along the road. Pass several turnings on the right, including White Hill and a turning to Burghclere. Continue beyond a cottage, with chickens and ducks roaming about freely. Swing half-left after a few yards and join a grassy track. In the top right corner of the field aim for an enclosed path. There is woodland on the right. Pass through several gates by some paddocks and then bear left by a cottage. Keep to the track as it cuts to the right of Nuthanger Farm. Soon it bends sharp right. Turn left just beyond the bend and follow a field track. On the right are magnificent views of Watership Down, one of North Hampshire's most famous landmarks. With its legendary associations, the reality of a visit to this lonely hillside does little to destroy the rare, magical quality of Richard Adams' book.

Keep to the track and soon you reach a field. Veer left along its edge and then make for a gap in the trees. Follow a woodland path between fields and eventually it broadens to a grassy ride cutting between hedgerows. At the road turn left and go up the slope for a few yards, until the road begins to descend towards Ecchinswell. Bear right at this point to a stile by a gate. Cross the field diagonally to the bottom corner of the field. Pass over another stile and then a footbridge. Walk along the left edge of the field, with glimpses of the houses of Ecchinswell across the fields. Pheasants may also be seen on this stretch of the walk.

Pass a footpath on the left and in the field corner cross a plank bridge over a ditch into the next field. Go straight across, towards a line of trees. On reaching a path on the far side of the field, beneath the trees, bear left and walk along the woodland

11

Ecchinswell's aquatic residents.

edge. Follow the line of a pretty stream and, as you approach the bridge, swing left to cross a stile into a delightful elongated field, fringed by woodland. Further on, look for another stile in the right-hand boundary and follow the path across the stream by means of a rustic wooden footbridge.

Continue through the line of trees, with the stream on your immediate left. The outline of Ecchinswell church is clearly visible on the right, its distinctive spire peeping above the trees. Keep on the path as far as the road, briefly following a track immediately before joining it. Turn left by the war memorial and walk back to the pub, in the centre of Ecchinswell.

2 Tangley
The Fox

Probably built as an inn about 300 years ago, the Fox is a popular pub, hidden in the isolated country of north-west Hampshire. The landlord pointed out one or two relics from bygone days, including several walls of exposed flint, black in places. At one time there used to be a bread oven at the back of the pub. The inside of the white-painted inn is small, cosy and intimate, with welcoming log fires in winter. Look out for a print of 'Mr Fox's hunt breakfast on Christmas Day' and one containing the history of various ales.

Food is served every day and includes such dishes as home-made soup, ploughman's, pâté, plaice and chips, chicken curry, steak and kidney pie – something of a speciality – chicken and mushroom pie, Coronation prawns, fillet steak and rump steak. Among other more substantial dishes, there is grilled lamb, Oriental duck and sirloin of beef. Vegetarian meals are also plentiful. Sticky toffee pudding is a popular favourite on the list of desserts. Half portions of some dishes are available for

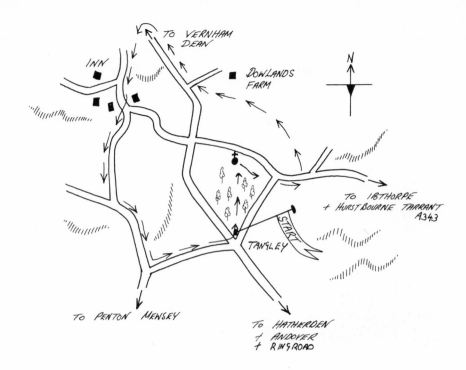

children. There is a good choice of drinks from the bar. Lagers include Kronenbourg, Carling Black Label and Carlsberg. The real ales consist of Bass, Royal Oak and Courage Best, and Strongbow draught cider is also available.

The Fox is open during the week and on Saturday between 11 am and 3 pm and 6 pm and 11 pm, and on Sunday the hours are between 12 noon and 3 pm and 7 pm and 10.30 pm. It is advisable to ring at weekends, especially for larger groups. Dogs on a lead, please. Bed and breakfast accommodation is also available.

Telephone: 0264 70276.

How to get there: Tangley lies north of Andover, to the west of the A343 Newbury road. From the ring road around Andover follow the signs for Charlton. Go through the village and on to Hatherden. About 1½ miles north of Hatherden you reach the Fox at a fork.

15

Tangley's historic church.

Parking: The main pub car park is at the rear of the inn.

Length of the walk: 3¼ miles. Map: OS Landranger 185 Winchester and Basingstoke (inn GR 334518).

This delightful walk explores the remote, undiscovered north-west corner of Hampshire, cutting through isolated tracts of countryside and along a network of quiet country lanes winding between trees and hedgerows, routes that seemingly go on for ever. A reminder that some parts of the south have not yet been consigned to the planner's axe.

The Walk

From the front of the inn turn left and walk up the lane towards Upton and Hurstbourne Tarrant. The lane soon enters mixed woodland. Immediately beyond Bramble Cottage on the left, bear left to join a clear, waymarked path cutting through the woodland. The track weaves between the trees, and in places it can be quite wet and muddy underfoot. Follow the track through the dense woodland and soon you reach a plantation on the left, enclosed by fencing.

Shortly the track arrives at Tangley church, St Thomas of Canterbury. The key is available at Church View. There is also a convenient seat here, in case you want to pause for a few moments and admire the quiet beauty of the church and its peaceful, rural surroundings. Yew trees surround this late 19th century place of worship, which contains the only lead font in Hampshire.

Turn right at this point and go down the lane between fields and trees. At the bottom of the slope you reach a junction. Continue ahead up the other side towards several cottages. When you draw level with a thatched cottage, turn left on to a waymarked path. The path, all that remains of an old Roman road known as Chute Causeway, running from the coast to Cirencester, is lined by holly bushes and trees. In places there are glimpses of rolling, semi-wooded countryside. The spire of Tangley church can be seen peeping above the trees over to the left. Now and again the sound of overhead aircraft will remind you that the military base at Middle Wallop is only a few miles away.

Continue on the path as it runs over high ground near the

Wiltshire border. There are good views on the right over a wide area of farmland. On the left are delightful, unspoilt vistas between the lines of trees. Distant hedgerows and the odd farm may be glimpsed. This stretch of the old Roman road is a perfect example of a peaceful walk in undisturbed surroundings, capturing the true spirit of the countryside.

In a while you reach the road at the point where it bends. Continue straight on and shortly you will see the entrance to Dowlands Farm on the right. To the south lie the hills of mid-Hampshire. Keep going, making for a line of trees ahead, where a footpath sign is visible. Bear left at the sign and follow the sunken path between ancient trees, including oak and holly, and fields.

At the fork swing left and continue on the muddy bridlepath between trees and fields. Soon you reach a barrier and at this point you join a concrete track running alongside some farm buildings. Further on, you arrive at the Cricketers Arms, once a drovers' inn – the last watering hole for shepherds driving their flocks south to Weyhill Fair. Note the whimsical 18th century epitaph:

'Here sleeps in peace a Hampshire Grenadier
Who caught his death by drinking cold, small beer.
Soldiers take heed from this untimely fall
And when you're hot drink Strong or not at all.'

At the junction walk ahead along the lane between some cottages and a wooden fence. After about 100 yards turn right by a letter-box. Pass a cute little thatched cottage on the left. Along this stretch of road are glimpses of distant rural horizons, as you look towards the countryside of mid-Hampshire.

Pass a set of ornately decorated wrought-iron gates leading to an imposing country mansion, set in peaceful parkland. Follow the lane as it curves to the left and then runs straight, between holly trees and hedgerows. At the junction bear left and then, after a few yards, follow the road round to the right. At the next bend, where there is a turning on the right, swing left and keep on the road through a landscape of fields and distant woodland. Descend the slope to a junction, then turn left and go back to the inn.

3 Monxton
The Black Swan

Probably the most unusual feature of this charming village inn is its ground floor design – the kitchens are at the front, the bars at the rear. It is also deceptively large. The Black Swan dates back to the 16th century. During the Second World War it was a regular haunt of many fighter pilots based at nearby Middle Wallop – it is understood that among them was the legendary war hero Douglas Bader.

The inn has a main bar, dining area and family room. At the rear is a garden and play area for children, which runs down to the river. The local wildlife is a popular attraction, ducks having been known to meander into the bar from time to time. There is also, unusually, a listed thatched wall at the back of the pub. The real ales include Wadworth 6X and Flowers IPA. Heineken, Stella Artois, Murphy's Irish Stout and Strongbow draught cider are also available. You can choose something to eat from a printed menu or from the daily specials board. Dishes include plaice, scampi, jumbo sausage, beefburger, toad in the hole,

19

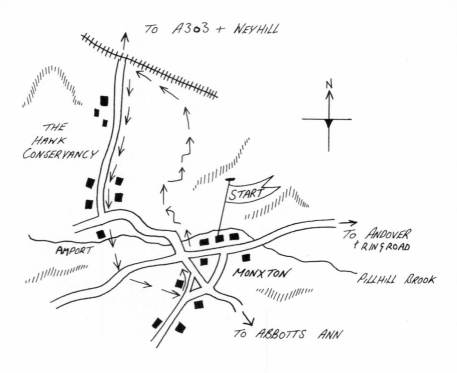

chilli, lasagne and cottage pie. There is a choice of jacket potatoes, as well as salads, ploughman's and sandwiches. On Sunday a traditional roast is served. A children's menu offers fish fingers, sausages and burgers, and vegetarians are also well catered for.

During the summer the inn is open all day – from 11 am until 11 pm and cream teas are available in the afternoon. On Sunday the hours are standard, from 12 noon to 3 pm and 7 pm to 10.30 pm. Winter opening hours are 11 am until 2.30 pm and 6 pm until 11 pm. The inn permits well-behaved dogs, preferably on a lead.

Telephone: 0264 710620.

How to get there: Monxton lies a couple of miles to the south-west of Andover. Using the ring road, follow the signs for the village. The Black Swan is on the right as you enter Monxton from Andover.

20

Parking: The Black Swan does not have a car park, but there is a parking area for patrons for the inn a few yards down the street. The main street of the village is narrow and not really suitable for parking.

Length of the walk: 3 miles. Map: OS Landranger 185 Winchester and Basingstoke (inn GR 314444).

The walk crosses the Pillhill Brook and then cuts across open fields to reach the famous Hawk Conservancy, which contains many different birds of prey, including eagles, owls, falcons, vultures and hawks. There are flying demonstrations every day from March to October – weather permitting. You can even be photographed with one of these hunters perched on your wrist! The route returns to Monxton mainly on tracks, with some spectacular views over the rolling countryside.

The Walk

From the inn turn right and walk along the road, bearing right towards Amport. Go over the Pillhill Brook, a tributary of the river Anton, and when the road bends left go straight on, by Corner Cottage, along the concrete road to Manor Farm. On the right are glimpses of Monxton church among the trees. At the next gate bear left to join a waymarked path. To the south are good views over the picturesque thatched roofs of Monxton village. Go through a kissing gate and walk along the edge of the field. In the corner disregard the next kissing gate and veer right, keeping the field boundary on your immediate left. In the top corner bear right and make for the stile in the next corner, completing three sides of the field in all. On the right you get a clear picture of Monxton, its pretty cottages sheltering in the semi-wooded valley. The church can be seen amid the trees.

Cross the stile into the next field and then turn left. Walk along the field edge, with the hedge on your left. This stage of the walk offers wide views over a spacious landscape close to the Wiltshire boundary. Follow the hedge round to the right, then left again after about 50 yards. The hedgerow is still on your left. Helicopters from the nearby base at Middle Wallop zip about the skies from time to time. Follow the clear, grassy path through the fields, its route quite obvious as it makes for a distant line of trees and some houses.

Owls may perch on your hand at the Hawk Conservancy.

Eventually you reach a curtain of brambles and bushes. There is an opening here and beyond it the path runs up to a footbridge over the railway line. Do not follow the path over the line, but continue along the field edge so that the railway and a row of houses are on the right. At the road turn left and follow the quiet country lane through this prairie-like patchwork of fields. Shortly you reach the entrance to the Hawk Conservancy on the right. For information on opening times, ring 0264 772252.

After a visit, continue along the road and soon you pass the entrance to some light engineering workshops on the right and a waymarked path on the left. Follow the lane towards the buildings of Amport, passing Sarson Close on the right and various bungalows and timber chalets on the left. Look for a delightful thatched cottage on the right and then at the junction, just beyond Cob Mews, turn left for about 25 yards.

Turn right on to a track and then recross the Pillhill Brook at a pretty spot. There are glimpses over lazy meadows towards groups of cottages. Follow the muddy track up the slope between trees and hedgerows. On the left you can see the houses of Monxton quite clearly.

22

At the road bear left for about 50 yards until you reach two waymarked paths. Disregard the first and join the next one. Follow the path, identified by a series of white marker posts, across the fields and here there are spectacular views across a wide, rolling landscape. Monxton is visible again, its church and cottages nestling in the valley. Draw level with some houses and then go through a hedge gap to the road. Bear left, and then left again at the next junction, by some thatched cottages. Walk down to the junction, turning right for the inn and car park.

4 Sparsholt
The Plough

The Plough is a spacious pub on the edge of Sparsholt village. There are good facilities for children, including a pleasant garden and a paddock. Donkeys and chickens are among the attractions. There is also a chalet in the garden, used as a children's room. Inside the pub is a popular dining area/family room. The oldest part of the Plough dates back about 250 years. It was originally a farmhouse, becoming an alehouse in the second half of the 18th century. These days it is a favourite among locals as well as customers from further afield, providing modern facilities and a welcoming atmosphere.

The Plough's menu is varied and interesting. 'Small eats' range from soup of the day to garlic baguette and baked goats' cheese. 'Large eats' include rich rabbit casserole, steak and kidney pudding, roast guinea fowl and fish and potato pie. The snack menu has a variety of freshly baked baguettes and brown doorstep sandwiches, jacket potatoes, omelettes and ploughman's lunches. The children's menu offers fish fingers, burgers and fries as well as marmite sandwiches. There is a traditional roast on Sunday. Among the real ales are Wadworth 6X and Henry's IPA. There is also Dry Blackthorn, Heineken and Kronenbourg. Dogs are welcome.

Times of opening are 11 am to 3 pm and 6.30 pm to 11 pm Monday to Friday and 11 am to 3 pm and 7 pm to 11 pm on Saturday. On Sunday the hours are 12 noon to 3 pm and 7 pm to 10.30 pm.

Telephone: 0962 776353.

How to get there: From Winchester head west towards Stockbridge on the A272. Once clear of the city outskirts look for the turning to Sparsholt on the left. The inn is on the right as you enter the village.

Parking: There is ample room to park at the pub. Limited spaces are also available in the village centre.

Length of the walk: 4 miles. Map: OS Landranger 185 Winchester and Basingstoke (inn GR 437314).

The middle stages of this varied and scenic walk are under cover of trees. The route passes through a delightful and ancient coppice on the edge of Farley Mount Country Park. The park itself extends to 1,000 acres of rich downland, ancient woodland and forestry plantation. It is a popular amenity area and has a wide variety of wildlife. The views over open countryside near the finish of this walk are some of the most striking in Hampshire.

The Walk

From the front of the inn turn left and walk up the lane towards Lainston House. At the first junction, where there is a sign 'Single file traffic', bear right and drop down the narrow lane between trees and hedgerows. There are good views over the rolling farmland of mid-Hampshire. Pass a waymarked footpath in the right-hand bank. Continue down beyond Dean Hill Cottage to the pretty hamlet of Dean, which consists of little more than a cluster of charming thatched cottages. As the road bends left by Barn Cottage, go straight on along a bridleway running between hedges and trees. Over on the left is a paddock. Beyond it you can see the houses of Dean.

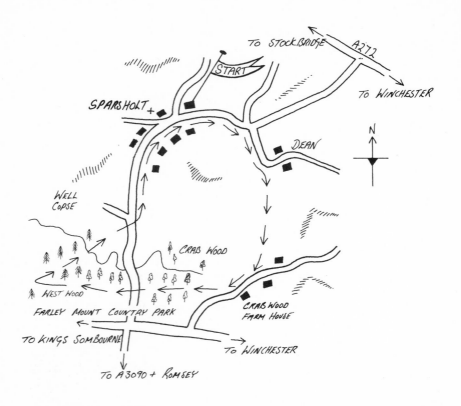

Head up the chalk slope and pass turnings on the left and right. The path runs through a tunnel of yew trees and soon passes a turning on the right. Continue on the main bridleway as it follows field edges all the way to the road.

Turn right and pass several remote houses and barns. There are striking views on the right, over a wide rural expanse. Soon the lane becomes enveloped by woodland. On your immediate right is a waymarked path running into the trees. Ignore the turning and continue along the lane. Pass a wide entrance to the wood further on and walk on down the road until you reach another main gateway. There is a 'no parking' sign here. Turn right at this point and follow the winding track through Crab Wood, all the way to the road. Crab Wood is an ancient hazel and oak coppice, rich in wild flowers and butterflies in summer.

At the road you meet the route of the Clarendon Way, a

25-mile waymarked path running from Salisbury to Winchester. The route is named after Clarendon Palace, a hunting lodge for Norman kings, near Salisbury. At the road go straight across and join the next section of the waymarked route. The path plunges deeper into the woods, muddy in places and clearly well used by horses. Keep to the main path, disregarding several turnings to the left and right. Eventually you reach a peaceful forest clearing. In front of you at this point is the Forestry Commission sign for West Wood.

To visit nearby Farley Mount Country Park – perhaps exploring its network of paths and trails, if there is time – turn left and continue on the Clarendon Way, returning to this junction afterwards.

With the Forestry Commission sign on your left, go straight on along the clear bridleway through the silver birch trees. Don't veer over to the track on the left or take the gated track on the right. Follow the bridleway as it heads for the north-east boundary of West Wood. Eventually the trees thin as you reach the outer edge of the woodland. The path now follows a strip of trees and bushes running between fields. On the left are fields

Donkeys grazing in the garden of the Plough.

and paddocks enclosed by the trees of West Wood and Well Copse. Horses may be seen here from time to time. After more than ½ mile on the bridlepath you join a track serving a number of bungalows where you may see chickens, geese and ducks roaming freely. Pass the entrance to Little Sheddons and, just before reaching the road junction, look for a path veering off half-left into the trees. Follow it down to the lane and bear left.

Soon the buildings of Sparsholt loom into view. The approach to the village offers some of the best views on the entire walk. Either side of the road are wide expanses of countryside and distant downland. Blustery, at times, and exhilarating.

In the centre of Sparsholt, pass the village memorial hall and the church and continue along the lane. The road is a little busy at peak times – so take care on this stretch. Follow the road round the right-hand bend and the inn is on the left.

5 Lockerley
The King's Arms

The inn lies close to the river Dun and the pretty village green at Lockerley. It is a straightforward village pub with a good atmosphere and a separate eating area away from the main bar. There are plenty of 'olde worlde' features, including exposed brickwork, beams and horse brasses. There is also a cosy log fire (in winter), and an old brewery sign on display 'Strong & Co of Romsey'.

The King's Arms, popular with fishermen, campers, walkers and visitors to the nearby New Forest, offers food every day except Wednesday. The bar menu includes a selection of ploughman's, sandwiches, light meals – such as ham, egg and chips, sausage and chips, chicken and chips and lasagne, chips and salad – and a range of other dishes, among them chicken Kiev, cod in batter and golden scampi. Jacket potatoes, filled with beans, ham, prawns, cheese or coleslaw, are also available. There is a popular specials board – steak and kidney pie and beef casserole with fresh vegetables are among the dishes that

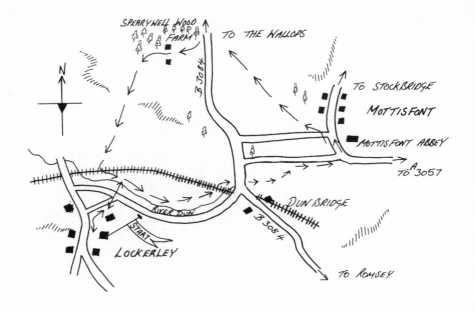

crop up quite regularly – and a children's menu offering, for example, chicken nuggets, sausages, ham and egg, and beefburgers. Cask-conditioned Strong Country Bitter and Ringwood Fortyniner will appeal to the real ale enthusiast, as will the other choices that take their place from time to time. Draught cider includes Inch's and Stonehouse. There is also a selection of various wines by the glass. Outside is a beer garden and a play area for children. Dogs must be well behaved and on a lead, please. Large groups are asked to book, especially at weekends.

The times of opening are weekdays from 11 am to 3 pm and 6 pm to 11 pm. On Saturdays and bank holidays the inn is open all day from 11 am until 11 pm. Sunday hours are from 12 noon to 3 pm and 7 pm to 10.30 pm.

Telephone: 0794 340332.

How to get there: From Romsey head north on the A3057 towards Stockbridge. Bear left on to the B3084 for Awbridge, then left in the village for Lockerley. The inn is on the right as you approach from Awbridge.

Parking: There is a car park at the inn.

Length of the walk: 4 miles. Map: OS Landranger 185 Winchester and Basingstoke (inn GR 302258).

There is much to see on this pleasant walk. Initially, the route follows the banks of the river Dun before making for Mottisfont Abbey, one of the great historic houses in this area. Beyond Mottisfont the walk enters thick woodland before returning to Lockerley.

The Walk

Leave the inn by turning right and walking along the road for about 70 yards. Swing half-right at some white railings, to join a lane which runs alongside the spacious village green. Pretty houses and cottages overlook the green. At the junction bear right and walk along the road for about 50 yards to a waymarked path on the left, just beyond Dunmeads. The path crosses the river Dun, a tributary of the Test. The Dun, one of Hampshire's lesser-known rivers, is especially pretty at this point, with weeping willows and various other trees trailing their branches in the water. The Dun was also known as 'the Barge river' for a time. This is a reference to the Salisbury Canal, an ambitious navigation intended to link the cathedral city with Southampton. The scheme was never completed.

Cross the footbridge and then turn immediately right, going over a stile and following a muddy path across a low-lying field. Cross several footbridges. The railway line is over to your left. Make for the stile up ahead in the far boundary. Cross it, then a footbridge over a ditch, into the next field. Begin to aim slightly right to a gap in the hedge, making for the right-hand side of the power cables. Join a path running through an area of rough grass and scrub.

Pass above a pretty, flowing stream running through a wooded hollow. Continue through the coarse grass to a thatched cottage. The path runs alongside the front of the cottage and then joins a track. Follow the track as it curves to the left and heads for the railway line. There is an electricity sub-station on the left. Go over the railway line at the crossing. About 100 yards to the right is the station at Dunbridge. Follow the track down to the road and then take the waymarked path opposite – signposted 'Mottisfont Abbey Garden'.

Follow the clear path through the crops. The houses of Dunbridge are visible down in the valley, near the point where the Dun flows into the Test. Head for a couple of trees on the side of a low hill, bearing left towards them and then, almost immediately, right. Follow the clear path across the higher ground of the field towards the houses of Mottisfont. There are good views to the north over the striking downland and country of mid-Hampshire.

Make for a solitary oak tree in the boundary and then follow the path between hedge and fence as far as the road. Bear right towards the village, following the narrow lane between high banks and hedgerows. Go down to the junction and note the charming little post office on the right. Teas and morning coffee are available here.

To visit Mottisfont Abbey, a National Trust property, turn right and walk down to the entrance. This was originally a 12th century Augustinian priory, before becoming a private house after the Dissolution. The Abbey includes a drawing room decorated by Rex Whistler and a superb walled garden containing one of the finest collections of roses in the country. A tributary of the nearby Test flows through the elegant grounds. Mottisfont Abbey and gardens are open to the public during the summer months. There is an admission charge.

To continue with the walk, bear left at this junction and pass some old farm buildings and stables. Turn left opposite one of the entrances to Mottisfont Abbey and walk along Bengers Lane for a few yards. Pass Abbey Farmhouse and then bear right, crossing a stile into a field. Head diagonally across the field towards a finger of woodland pointing east. There are memorable views from here back to Mottisfont and across the Test valley. The quarry works at Michelmersh can also be spotted.

Go through a gap in the trees by a waymarker post and head for the next field via a footbridge. The path cuts diagonally across the field but it is easier to follow its right-hand edge to avoid the mud. Exit from the field through some double gates and go out to the road.

If time allows, you may want to stroll along to the entrance to Spearywell Wood, part of the National Trust's Mottisfont

Mottisfont Abbey.

Estate. You can walk among the trees here, enjoying the welcome shade on a warm day. Return to the road and head back to the double gates, through which you passed on the walk.

Turn right to join a track running alongside a house and follow it through the trees. Soon the track emerges from the trees and cuts across open fields to reach Cadbury Farm. When you arrive at the farmhouse, with its south-facing verandah, go straight on down towards the woodland, following a stony track. Go through the barrier and then bear immediately left, just inside the cover of the trees. Follow the path down between plantations and more mature woodland. There are banks of brambles and undergrowth, and various species of tree, including oak and silver birch. This is one of the highlights of the walk – a pleasant, undisturbed woodland scene.

Eventually, the path reaches a major junction. Turn left and walk along a stony track, with a field on your left. After about 70 yards you reach another barrier. Swing right, just inside the trees, and follow a path carpeted with pine cones and needles. At the corner of the woodland go over a stile and follow a path between fences and hedges. On the right are views of rising downland, stretching beyond the Wiltshire border. The spire of Lockerley church rises above the trees. Follow the path through some pretty woodland, with a stream meandering below you. This low-lying stretch of the walk can be extremely muddy underfoot. Pass through the railway arch, re-cross the Dun and go out to the road. Turn right, then left at the green and return to the King's Arms.

6 Canterton
The Sir Walter Tyrrell

This well-known inn is situated in a peaceful corner of the New Forest, close to the villages of Brook and Cadnam. Originally the pub was sited nearby and was known as the Stump, named after the one-legged landlady who ran it. It became the Sir Walter Tyrrell in 1929 but was destroyed by fire after the Second World War. The inn was rebuilt and today it is a thriving family hostelry with a welcoming atmosphere and a good reputation for food. Families can eat in the informal dining area or in the restaurant. There is also a pub garden which includes many amusements for children – among them swings, climbing frames and a summertime paddling pool. The patio is a popular feature and on summer weekends the inn can get very busy. Dogs are welcome.

The 'Farmhouse Kitchen' menu is comprehensive and includes a selection of starters, such as garlic bread and prawn cocktail. Hot platters include Cumberland sausage and curry. There is a selection of ploughman's, vegetarian dishes and

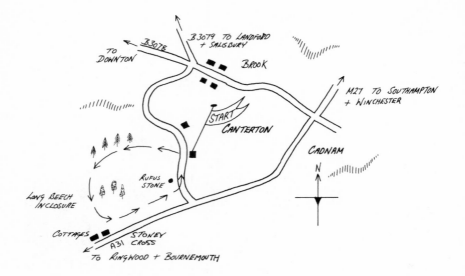

hoagies – a French stick with various fillings – as well as a children's menu and a traditional Sunday roast. The inn also has a speciality fish board, with mussels as a constant favourite. The real ales include Directors, Ruddles County and a guest ale. There is also Strongbow and Scrumpy Jack draught cider and Kronenbourg, Foster's and Holsten Export.

Between June and August the inn is open from 11 am to 11 pm on Monday to Saturday. The rest of the year the hours are 11 am to 3 pm and 7 pm to 11 pm. On Sundays throughout the year the hours are 12 noon to 3 pm and 7 pm to 10.30 pm. It is a good idea for families to book.

Telephone: 0703 813170.

How to get there: Canterton is just off the A31 and is near to Cadnam and junction 1 of the M27. The easiest route from here is north towards Brook and Bramshaw. At the junction at Brook (near the Green Dragon) take the lane on the extreme left (not the B3078) and follow it towards the Rufus Stone. The inn is on the left.

Parking: There is a roomy car park at the pub. You can also park at the nearby Rufus Stone.

Length of the walk: 2 miles. Map: OS Landranger 195 Bournemouth and district (inn GR 268127).

This is a short walk highlighting the beauty and ancient history of the New Forest. The route cuts between lines of trees, wild plants and herbs. There is a gentle climb and from the higher ground there are far-reaching views over the forest. Further on, in a peaceful clearing, is the Rufus Stone — recalling one of the great, unsolved mysteries of the New Forest.

The Walk

From the Sir Walter Tyrrell go out to the road and across to the expanse of spongy turf. Aim half-right and pass over several little streams. Make for a gap in the trees and cross over the shallow ford. Walk straight ahead towards a line of power cables and, on reaching them, bear left and head south towards the trees, following the line of the cables.

Continue on the clear path between holly bushes and silver birch trees. In wet weather it can be hard going on this stretch, the ground saturated by rain. However, there is an easier alternative route running parallel through the trees on the right, where the ground is usually quite dry even after rain. The path climbs gently and on this stretch you may see clumps of a wild plant known as butchers broom. Gypsies pick it and spray it with gold, selling it as a lucky charm. Look out for dog myrtle, a wild herb, and blackthorn, its white flowers and dark stems instantly recognisable in spring.

As you approach the crest of the hill, traffic is audible on the nearby A31. On the higher ground pass beneath the cables and then veer half-left amid clumps of gorse bushes. Look for the roof and chimney of a cottage peeping through the trees near the road. Pass over a cross track and continue towards the cottage. Go on as far as some holly bushes. The main road is just ahead of you. At the clear track bear left and begin to head east. The A31 is parallel on the right. This part of the walk provides distant views over the New Forest.

Follow the track and soon the outline of the television booster mast comes into view on the horizon. When you reach a track running off sharp left by a manhole cover, aim half-left across the scrub to join another track running through the trees. Continue in an easterly direction with the booster half-right.

Rufus Stone.

Soon the track curves to the left and goes on to reach the road by a barrier.

Turn left and walk down the lane between lines of trees. Further down, the car park for the Rufus Stone looms into view. Opposite it is the stone – one of the New Forest's most famous and historic attractions. It is claimed that King William Rufus, son of William the Conqueror, was accidentally killed by an arrow shot by the nobleman Sir Walter Tyrrell while out hunting in Canterton Glen in the summer of 1100. He had supposedly meant to kill a stag but the arrow glanced and struck Rufus, the most hated of kings. The body lay where it fell and was eventually discovered by a charcoal burner who carried it on a cart to Winchester. According to some sources, the shooting was not an accident and there is a suggestion that the incident took place elsewhere in the New Forest. But whether it took place here or somewhere else, it is a fascinating tale of mystery and royal intrigue. The forest setting has changed little since the death of Rufus and, with a little imagination, it is possible to picture the circumstances surrounding his demise. The memorial stone marking the spot is encased in iron and was erected in 1841.

Continue along the road and after a short distance you reach the inn where the walk began.

7 Linwood
The High Corner Inn

Its isolated forest location at the bottom of an old drovers' track is one of the inn's main attractions. It is a classic pub for families, who come from miles around to this popular venue. The building dates back to the 1700s but was extensively rebuilt in the 1980s, following a fire. There are excellent facilities for families, with plenty of indoor seating. The High Corner offers accommodation as well. In summer there is a barbecue most Saturday evenings. Children can choose from a wide selection of amusements – among them is a bouncy castle, an indoor Lego/Duplo room and various video games. Dogs are also welcome.

There is an à la carte restaurant and a wide selection of bar meals. Dishes include local game pâté, crisp garlic mushrooms and freshly prepared soup, as well as a choice of fish, vegetarian meals, ploughman's and sandwiches. There is also tagliatelle, home-made beef, kidney and mushroom pie and 8 oz gammon steak. Several grills are available and roast lemon chicken with coleslaw and garlic dip. A specials board offers further choices. On Sunday there is a traditional roast. Children are catered for with a choice of fish fingers and chicken nuggets, among other dishes. The real ales include Flowers IPA and Wadworth 6X. There is also Heineken, Stella Artois, Guinness and Dry Blackthorn and Autumn Gold draught cider.

The times of opening are Monday to Saturday from 11 am to 3 pm and 6 pm to 11 pm and on Sunday from 12 noon to 3 pm and 7 pm to 10.30 pm. The inn is open all day on Saturday in summer.

Telephone: 0425 473973.

How to get there: From Cadnam, at the start of the M27, head north on the B3079 and then join the B3078 at Brook. Turn left (signposted 'Fritham'), then right (signposted 'Linwood'). Follow the road round to the right and look for the turning to High Corner. Go down the track to the inn.

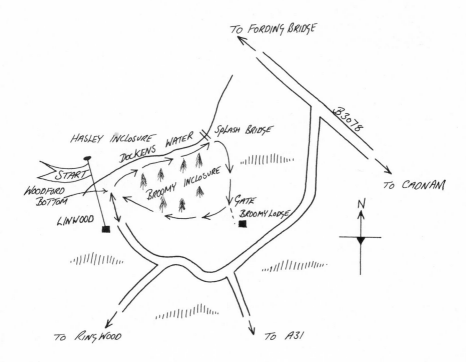

Walkers at Broomy Inclosure in the New Forest.

Parking: There is a car park at the inn. The pub's remote setting in the forest makes parking at the High Corner the most obvious choice.

Length of the walk: 2½ miles. Map: OS Landranger 195 Bournemouth and district (inn GR 196108).

This walk takes you deep into the heart of the New Forest. For some time the route follows the Dockens Water, running alongside the dense woodland of Broomy Inclosure. The trees are a constant delight, creating a rich blend of hues and acting as a thick, protective curtain. When I undertook this walk in the spring, I saw horses and grazing ponies, I heard woodpeckers in the trees and saw carpets of bluebells and foxgloves. It is an ideal short walk, offering something for everyone.

The Walk

Make for the 'Forestry Commission inn car park' sign and bear left, heading down the track with the High Corner Inn now on your left. After a few yards veer right at the fork and pass between the trees. There is much evidence of dead wood either side of the track. Soon a picturesque thatched cottage comes into view on the left. Over to the right beyond the grassy clearing are the trees of Broomy Inclosure.

Continue down the track and when it sweeps to the left, bear right and follow it into the trees. Pass the Forestry Commission sign for 'Woodford Bottom' and after about 100 yards, as the track approaches another gate, veer off half-left into the trees. After several yards swing right and walk along a path, with the Dockens Water, a shallow New Forest brook, close by on your left. In high summer this is an idyllic spot – the cool air of the stream and the gentle breeze in the branches of the trees helping to ease the burnishing heat of the sun. In the winter months the going can be slow here, after heavy rain. On your right are the trees of Broomy Inclosure, lines of conifers and beech growing in thick profusion. Glancing between the regulated rows you can spot shafts of daylight, but such is the density and concentration of trees that even on the brightest, sunniest day the scene amid the tangle of branches is dark – it is like something from the pages of a children's classic.

Lunch in the New Forest.

Continue beyond a gate (numbered '94') on the right. The Dockens Water is still visible over on the left, winding through the forest. Scots pine can be seen beside the path. To the north, beyond the water, are glimpses of Hasley Inclosure and Sloden Inclosure. Look for Splash Bridge over to the left now. At this point you bear right at the corner of Broomy Inclosure and follow a track running alongside oak woodland.

After about 100 yards you come to a gate on the right. Go through it to join a broad woodland ride, cutting between the trees of Broomy Inclosure. Larch trees add a distinctive hue to the rich, multi-coloured canopy of colours and in spring a carpet of bluebells creates a hazy blue tint in the woodland. Cross over a junction of tracks close to some silver birch trees and carry on beside beech woodland and bracken clearings. I heard the distinctive sound of the woodpecker on this stretch of the walk.

Soon you reach the gate at Woodford Bottom. You can either return to the inn by the same route along the track or take a short cut by cutting across the turf on the left and aiming for the pretty, thatched cottage seen near the start of this walk. Follow the track back to the inn at High Corner.

8 Brockenhurst
The Rose and Crown

Situated on the main A337 in Brockenhurst, the Rose and Crown is a rambling old coaching inn and hotel, dating back to the 18th century. It is also a Grade II listed building. The pub offers its customers a wide range of facilities. Apart from the bar, there is a spacious buffet, an à la carte restaurant and a family room, which includes video games and other amusements. There is also a skittle alley, for which it is a good idea to book.

The choice of home-cooked food is extensive and includes children's portions. The salads are many and various – crab, prawn, beef and mackerel among them. Sandwiches are available at lunchtime. There is also lasagne, fisherman's pie, chicken breast wrapped in bacon, steak and ale pie, steak and kidney pie, a selection of ploughman's and a range of American-style ¼ lb burgers, including hamburger, cheeseburger, bacon and cheese burger and chilli burger. Also on offer are Mexican specialities, steaks, fish and pizza dishes and a range of starters and light snacks. On Sunday there is a popular roast. The real

45

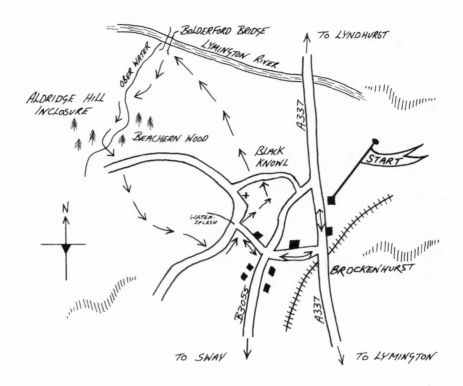

ales include Eldridge Pope's Hardy Country Bitter, Royal Oak and Dorchester Bitter. For the lager drinker there is a choice of Castlemaine XXXX, Kronenbourg and Carlsberg. Dry Blackthorn cider is also available. Outside is a most attractive beer garden, which is an extremely popular feature in summer. Dogs are permitted, though not in the eating areas.

The times of opening are Monday to Saturday from 11 am to 11 pm, and on Sunday from 12 noon to 3 pm and 7 pm to 10.30 pm.

Telephone: 0590 22225.

How to get there: Brockenhurst is easy to find. It lies on the main A337 Lyndhurst to Lymington road. The Rose and Crown is on the left coming from Lyndhurst just beyond a turning on the right to Sway.

46

Parking: There is a car park at the inn. There is also a free car park in Brookley Road and spaces elsewhere in Brockenhurst.

Length of the walk: 4¾ miles. Maps: OS Landranger 195 Bournemouth and district and 196 Solent and the Isle of Wight (inn GR 303024 on sheet 196).

Brockenhurst is one of the most popular centres within the New Forest. The name means 'the badger's wood' and the glorious riverside woods encountered on this walk make an ideal retreat for this little-seen creature. As well as following the described route through the forest clearings and along the banks of the Lymington river and the Ober Water, you can stroll the streets of Brockenhurst. Don't miss the churchyard monument to Brusher Mills, a renowned local character and snake catcher who died in 1905.

The Walk

From the Rose and Crown bear left and walk along the A337 until you come to Brookley Road. Turn right and follow it down to the shops and the watersplash at the junction with Rhinefield Road. Bear right here and follow the railings alongside the stream. When they end, continue beyond several bridges leading to various private properties. Then veer right on to a narrow path between the entrances to Brookway and Chadwicks.

Follow the path along the left bank of the stream. The setting is pretty here, with overhanging trees and glimpses of private gardens on the opposite bank. Pass through a gate to reach a lane (Butts Lawn) and a second watersplash. Turn left and follow the lane to a junction, with a 'phone box on the corner.

Bear left and then almost immediately right, signposted 'Access to Allotments'. Pass over a stream and then begin to veer a little to the right across a broad expanse of heath, known as Black Knowl. There is a belt of woodland on the horizon and a curtain of trees to the right, bordering the open heath. Keep the trees on your right and aim roughly for the far right corner. On reaching a wide stony track, turn right and walk the short distance to Bolderford Bridge. This pleasant tree-shaded spot is where the Lymington river meets Ober Water, a typical New Forest stream.

If time permits you may wish to stroll a little way along the

The watersplash at Brockenhurst.

northern bank of the Lymington river passing under oaks and beeches. Over on the left here is New Park, where deer can sometimes be seen amid the trees. Retrace your steps back over the bridge and follow the track round to the right.

Continue on the track, with Ober Water now on the right. When you reach the next junction keep on ahead along the metalled road between the trees. Soon you come to a turning on the right signposted 'Aldridge Hill'. Take the turning, cross Ober Water and then, after a few yards, take the path on the left running through the trees. Follow the path through the woodland, with Ober Water over on the left. Cross it at the next wooden footbridge and follow the path through the trees. Soon the route is bordered by rows of pines. Keep to the path until you reach the road on a corner.

Proceed ahead, with expanses of heath on the right. Pass Beachern Wood car park on the right and continue to the main junction. Here, turn right and then left just beyond Ober Lodge. Follow the track, with good views on the right of the woodland at Hinchelsea in the distance. Keep on the drive, passing a variety of properties on the left, Coronation Cottage and The

Willows among them. The drive twists and turns between trees and hedges. There are frequent unspoilt glimpses of the forest along this stretch. Eventually you reach the Burley road.

Bear left and follow the grass verge on the opposite side of the road, back to the watersplash at Brookley Road and then return to the inn.

Alternatively, take a short optional detour, avoiding much of the road. Opposite Armstrong Lane join a well-defined path, cross a footbridge and, as you begin to approach the primary school and main road, swing left over to a concrete bridge and head back to the Burley road, keeping the ditch and trees on the right. Turn right and, at the watersplash, bear right into Brookley road and then left at the A337 to the Rose and Crown.

9 Milford on Sea
The White Horse

The White Horse, located in Milford's long main street, is a spacious, comfortable old pub, dating back to the mid 18th century. It has lots of character and among the features are a wealth of beams and a cosy, warming fire in winter. As well as the bar area, there is an intimate little family room leading out to a sunny conservatory, very popular in summer. The White Horse attracts lots of customers – a happy mixture of locals and holidaymakers. Dogs are welcome at the inn and there is an enclosed area of garden outside, where children can let off steam in safety.

The food is good and there are always a lot of dishes to choose from. Traditional bar meals include a range of salads, sandwiches, jacket potatoes and ploughman's. There is a choice of starters, such as soup of the day, prawn cocktail and pâté and toast. Main meals include 8 oz sirloin steak, home-made chicken and mushroom pie, scampi, plaice, haddock, chicken curry, chilli con carne and jumbo sausage. Vegetarians are catered for and among the dishes are vegetable lasagne and crispy pancakes filled with vegetables and served with sweet and sour sauce and rice. There is also a children's menu which includes sausage and chips, fish fingers and battered chicken burger. The real ales at the White Horse include Boddingtons Bitter, Flowers Original, Young's Special and Ringwood Best. There is also Guinness and Strongbow draught cider and a choice of lager, including Heineken and Stella Artois.

The times of opening are from 11 am to 3 pm and 6 pm to 11 pm on Monday to Thursday, and 12 noon to 3 pm and 7 pm to 10.30 pm on Sunday. The pub is open all day, 11 am to 11 pm, on Friday and Saturday.

Telephone: 0590 642360.

How to get there: From Lymington head west on the A337 towards Bournemouth and Christchurch. Turn left, signposted

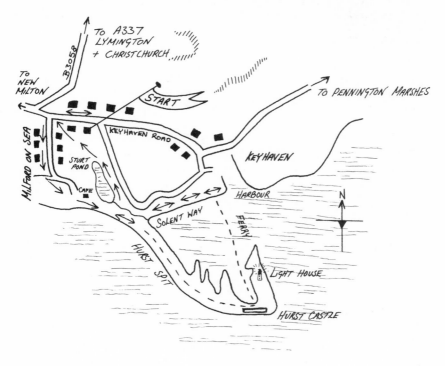

The Isle of Wight and the Needles beyond the Solent.

to Milford and Keyhaven, and when you reach the green at Milford bear sharp left to join the Keyhaven road. The White Horse is along this road on the right.

Parking: There is a spacious car park at the back of the inn. In nearby Sea Road there is a large public car park.

Length of the walk: 3 miles, or 4½ miles if you decide to include Hurst Castle. Map: OS Landranger 196 Solent and The Isle of Wight (inn GR 293917).

This walk offers outstanding views of the Solent and the Isle of Wight. You can follow the Solent Way to Keyhaven and then return via a pretty lagoon known as Sturt Pond, or, if you are feeling energetic, there is an optional spur along Hurst Spit to Hurst Castle and its neighbouring lighthouse. During the summer you can return to Keyhaven by ferry. On a sunny day the coastal scenery and the tangy ozone of the Solent add an extra dimension to this invigorating walk.

The Walk

From the White Horse turn left and walk along the Keyhaven road towards the centre of Milford on Sea. Soon you come to Sea Road. Bear left here and immediately on the left is a car park and a sign for the Solent Way. Ignore this at this stage of the walk and continue along Sea Road.

Follow the road between detached houses, many of them holiday villas and retirement homes. On the right is the entrance to the War Memorial Hospital. At the next junction (Hurst Road) turn left and walk along towards Marine Café. On the left are rows of holiday villas and private residences, all of which have magnificent views of the Solent, the Needles and the ridge of the Isle of Wight – a classic coastal view, reproduced in thousands of postcards, books and calendars and probably one of the most photographed scenes in the country.

Beyond the café walk ahead towards Hurst Spit. On the left is the outline of Sturt Pond. Pass a footbridge over a channel of water known as Danes Stream and continue to the next footbridge, where you are faced with a choice of routes. You can either walk to Keyhaven on the Solent Way or extend the route along Hurst Spit (see below).

If you are not planning a visit to Hurst Castle, cross the bridge to the road. Walk ahead along the road and then follow the parallel track to Keyhaven. The colourful harbour is a striking feature of this walk, bustling with boat activity and visiting tourists. There are good views across the marshes and mudflats to the Isle of Wight. Ornithologists flock to the area in search of its migratory birds. There is an inn, the Gun, where you may wish to stop for a drink, and the option of extending the walk by heading along the Solent Way and then back to Keyhaven across Pennington Marshes. Return to the footbridge near Sturt Pond by the same route.

Once over the footbridge bear right and walk along to the next footbridge. Cross it and then follow the Solent Way in an anti-clockwise direction round the edge of Sturt Pond, a favourite haunt of curlews, oystercatchers, reed warblers and herons. Over to your left, beyond the pond, are glimpses of Milford's pre and post-war residential development, much of it populated by holidaymakers and the retired. On the right holiday caravans line the path.

The spur to Hurst Castle offers magnificent coastal views.

Pass a footpath on the right and continue along the route of the Solent Way. The path hugs the reed beds – a silent wilderness in the midst of densely populated coastal conurbations. Soon the path reaches a road. Walk ahead for a few yards until you reach another stretch of path. Cross the Danes Stream at the bridge and then you arrive at the car park in the centre of Milford. Go out to Sea Road, turn right and then right again at the junction. The White Horse is a short distance along Keyhaven road on the right.

Optional spur to Hurst Castle: This extends the described walk by about 1 ½ miles. It is ideal for a summer's day when cool sea breezes provide relief from the sun. Pick a time when there is low tide – this enables you to walk along the sand rather than on the uncomfortable shingle bank which can be arduous at times and difficult for smaller children.

The spit is a curious geological quirk, a relic of the days when the Isle of Wight was attached to the mainland. A bleak sense of isolation surrounds this coastal fort. Stranded at the far end of the spit, alongside the distinctive 19th century lighthouse, it looks from Milford to be almost part of the Isle of Wight. The

54

width of the Solent between the fort and the island is so narrow that at times it assumes the appearance of a broad river.

Built in 1541 by Henry VIII to defend the western entrance to the Solent against French and Spanish attack, Hurst Castle is now in the care of English Heritage and is open to the public daily during the summer months between 10 am and 5.30 pm. During the rest of the year it is only open at weekends (10 am to 4 pm). There is a gift shop and a café. A ferry service operates between May and September. Make sure that you don't miss the last ferry back to Keyhaven – if you do, it means having to walk back along the spit!

Once the ferry has returned you to Keyhaven, follow the main route description for this walk, back to the White Horse at Milford.

Warsash
The Silver Fern

Located in a residential road near the old village centre, the Silver Fern is an ideal venue for families. Originally a transport café, it is especially popular with walkers on the Solent Way, holidaymakers and, above all, those who like a pub with spacious surroundings, a family room and plenty of amusements. Children have the chance to play on giant draughts and chess boards in the garden, or be entertained by a game of miniature golf. There are also swings, a slide and garden puzzles to enjoy. In wet weather children can try the indoor Duplo table, soft play area and blackboards or watch kids' TV programmes all day!

For the adults there is a choice of six real ales, which change regularly, and several lagers, including Heineken Export and Stella Artois. For cider drinkers there is Strongbow and Scrumpy Jack. The menu includes home-made lasagne, steak and kidney pie, chilli, beef curry and rice, various sandwiches and speciality dishes. There is also the Silver Fern Super Hot

Dog, as well as a selection of vegetarian meals, a specials board and a children's menu.

The pub is open all day, from 11 am to 11 pm, from Monday to Saturday. On Sunday the opening times are 12 noon to 3 pm and 7 pm to 10.30 pm. Dogs are welcome, but in the garden only.

Telephone: 0489 572057.

How to get there: Warsash is south of the M27 (junction 9) and the A25 Southampton to Fareham road. The village is signposted. The inn is in Warsash Road, just to the east of the shops, the roundabout and the clock tower.

Parking: There is a car park at the inn. Spaces may also be found down in the old village centre, overlooking the Hamble.

Length of the walk: 3¾ miles. Map: OS Landranger 196 Southampton and the Isle of Wight (inn GR 496063).

Beyond the Hook-with-Warsash Nature Reserve the splendid expanse of Southampton Water dominates the second half of this walk. Views of it will, for some, evoke memories of the great days of the ocean-going liners. There is plenty to see on the water all year round. The walk returns to the historic village of Warsash along a stretch of the invigorating Solent Way.

The Walk

From the inn car park turn left, cross to the opposite pavement and walk along the road. Continue ahead at the fork, into Dibles Road. The road undulates between residential houses and retirement bungalows. Further on, beside the road, is a pretty thatched cottage – a reminder that, until earlier this century, this was a rural and undeveloped corner of Hampshire. On the right of the road is an area of commonland where gorse, wild flowers, laurel bushes, trees and vegetation grow in profusion.

Pass the entrance to 'Dibles Residential and Touring Caravan Park' on the left. Beyond it you reach a junction with New Road, Fleetend Road and Fleetend Bottom. Turn right, down Fleetend Road, with the common on your right. On the left is a row of houses and bungalows. The road passes under some trees and crosses a bridge over a stream known as Hook Lake.

57

Colour washed cottages at Warsash.

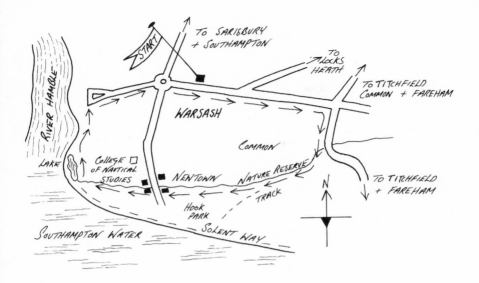

Immediately beyond it, bear right to join a waymarked waterside path running through the woodland. Gradually the path begins to climb between lines of holly trees. Suddenly the trees thin and the path runs alongside a paddock. Cross a stile and continue along a track between houses and their extensive gardens.

Follow the track round to the left and then turn right at the junction by a thatched cottage. Walk along the track. There are pleasant views over woodland and common to the right. Pass a track on the left and continue on the main drag. A little further on, just before the entrance to a private residence, there is a path on the right, running down through the trees to a gate. On reaching it bear left and immediately you come to a fork. Take the left-hand branch and follow the path as it runs just inside the woodland boundary. Emerge from the trees on to the edge of a playing field and continue along the right-hand edge, with the trees over to your right. Look for a gate in the far right corner of the field. Just before it is a gap in the hedgerow with a sign, 'Alternative Route'. Go through the gap and then bear left along the wide woodland path. This is the Hook valley – part of the Hook-with-Warsash Nature Reserve.

Go through a gate and continue down to the road. On the

right is the outline of the College of Nautical Studies. Cross the road and continue on the next stage of the walk, following a track beside some woodland. There is a row of substantial pre-war residences on the left. Just beyond the entrance to Christmas House join a narrow path running through the nature reserve. Go over a stile and follow the path as it bends right. Either side of you are banks of undergrowth and lines of trees.

Eventually, you reach the edge of Southampton Water – the dramatic coastal scenery here is in sharp contrast to the hitherto wooded, enclosed surroundings of the walk. With good visibility you can see the Isle of Wight, Calshot Castle and, nearer to hand, across the bustling expanse of Southampton Water, Fawley power station and oil refinery. This dramatic backdrop of pipes, chimneys and storage tanks often assumes the appearance of some sinister futuristic city from a science fiction film.

Follow the path as it bends right and then right again, heading inland now towards Warsash, the mouth of the Hamble and the College of Nautical Studies. The walk now follows the Solent Way, a 60-mile coastal path. The path is clear and well trodden as it runs across the freshwater marshes and close to Hook Lake. This part of the walk is a favourite haunt of wildlife and the shingle beach fringing Southampton Water contains various plants – sea campion and sea plantain among them. At the next junction bear left and walk along the Solent Way, with a wooden fence on your right. There are very good views over Southampton Water and the river Hamble. Pass a sign for 'Southampton Institute – Warsash Campus' and cross a slipway running down to the water's edge.

Continue on the waterside walk and pass a footpath on the right. The ground rises gently now and there is a welcome seat overlooking this spectacular scene. The cottages of Warsash come into view ahead, their colourful shutters standing out with some clarity. Walk along to the car parking area by the Rising Sun Inn. This is true Warsash – the genuine old village. Not much of the old crab and lobster fishing community survives but what remains is quite quaint. These days, of course, Warsash is more commonly known as one of this country's most popular sailing centres.

A commemorative plaque recalls that British and Allied Naval and Commando Units sailed from the Hamble river on the night of 5th June 1944 for the D-Day landings on the Normandy beaches.

Walk up the lane alongside the Rising Sun and head for the roundabout at the top. The most striking feature in this part of the village is the old clock tower, originally built as a water tower. At the roundabout go straight over into Warsash Road and back to the pub.

11 Rowland's Castle
The Robin Hood

The Robin Hood occupies a striking position overlooking the green at Rowland's Castle. Built as a row of cottages over 300 years ago, it was converted to a pub in the Victorian era, but still retains the air of a private house. Inside, there are several bars, a function room and a family room. Outside, at the front, is a small garden.

The real ales change regularly but Marston's Pedigree Bitter and Eldridge Pope Royal Oak are among the most popular. For cider drinkers there is Gaymers and Olde English, while for lager drinkers there is Lowenbrau, Carlsberg and Castlemaine XXXX. Fish is a speciality at the Robin Hood, with lemon sole, plaice fillet, baked cod fillet, very large brill, grilled sardines, dressed crab salad, bass and scampi wholetail, among other dishes. Alternatively, you could choose from a range of jacket potatoes and ploughman's, or go for steak, kidney and Guinness pie, chilli and rice, meatballs in creamy cheese, beef and mushroom casserole or chicken Kiev. There is also a choice of toasted and plain sandwiches and a traditional Sunday roast. The children's menu includes sausages and chicken nuggets.

The pub is open for business from 11 am to 2.30 pm and 6 pm to 11 pm on Monday to Thursday and from 11 am to 11 pm on Friday and Saturday. On Sunday the hours are 12 noon to 3 pm and 7 pm to 10.30 pm. No dogs, please. Telephone: 0705 412268.

How to get there: Rowland's Castle lies east of the A3(M) and just off the B2149 Havant to Horndean road. Follow signs for the village and make for the green.

Parking: There is a car park at the inn. Alternatively, there are usually some spaces in the vicinity of the Robin Hood, beside the green.

Length of the walk: 3¾ miles. Map: OS Landranger 197 Chichester and the Downs (inn GR 733107).

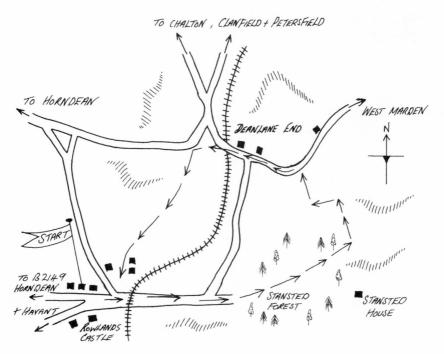

*In the 14th century Rowland's Castle is understood to have been called
'Rolokscastel'. There was a Norman castle here but a few mounds in a private
garden are all that remains of this site.*

*The walk cuts through nearby Stansted Forest — a peaceful haven of trees,
plants and wildlife. Stansted was a medieval hunting forest and in the late 12th
century Richard the Lionheart is believed to have hunted here. The walk
crosses into West Sussex at one point and then returns to Rowland's Castle
over high ground, with magnificent views in all directions.*

The Walk

From the inn bear left in front of the expansive green and walk
along the road and under the railway bridge. Pass the Castle Inn
on the left and the entrance to Stansted Park on the right.
Follow the brick and flint wall on the right and, when the road
bears left by the sign 'Finchdean Road', turn right into Stansted
Park. There is another sign here, 'dogs under control – no
picnicking'.

This is a delightful area of ancient, semi-natural broad-leaved
woodland. Species include oak, beech and chestnut. The forest
dates back to the Roman occupation. It was the site of a hunting
lodge, built for the 1st Earl of Arundel in the 11th century. The
house is now the home of the 10th Earl and Countess of
Bessborough and is situated in parkland which is part of the
Forest of Bere. The forest once covered a band of countryside
from Southampton to the Sussex border. In the 11th century it
was made a Royal Forest by William the Conqueror, but little
remains of it today, apart from occasional patches of woodland.
The main house and grounds are open to the public between
Easter and September. The days of the aristocracy, the great
landowning families and their inherited wealth are well
illustrated at Stansted, as is domestic life 'below stairs'.

Walk along the path for about 100 yards until you reach a
junction. Bear left to follow a well-trodden track. When it bends
left, continue ahead on the waymarked path and look for a
signposted track running off half-left after a few yards. Follow
it through the trees. After some time you come to a junction
with a wide woodland ride. Bear left for several yards, then
swing right and rejoin the woodland on the next stage of
the walk.

Avoid any turnings off into the trees and stay on the main

Stansted Forest where Richard the Lionheart hunted.

path. Further on, you break cover from the trees to cross another broad forest ride. Glancing to the right you will glimpse the distant outline of the great house, framed by trees.

Continue on the path as it enters another area of woodland and pass over a major junction of paths. Follow the waymarked path as far as the next junction and then bear left and left again after a few yards, at the next waymarker post. After several yards the path swings right at another signpost and heads down the slope, between the trees. Cross the route of another track and go on down to a stile. Cross it, into the field, and then head straight for the next stile in the opposite boundary. Go up the bank for several yards and then bear left by the garden of a flint cottage.

Follow the path along the edge of the field. Soon you reach another stile. Beyond it you continue down the field boundary. Disregard the next stile further down on the left and swing right for a few yards to another stile. Cross it and head up the slope of the field to a gate in the top boundary. A stile takes you out to the road by the 'Forestside' sign. This is a quiet rural hamlet. Turn left and walk down the road through the trees. Further on, the trees thin to reveal wide views over spacious, rolling countryside. This is border country, a landscape of fields, trees and hedgerows, interspersed with only the occasional cottage.

Follow the road round to the right, towards Deanlane End. Bear right, signposted 'Petersfield' and 'Finchdean'. Cross the county boundary dividing Hampshire and West Sussex and pass under the railway bridge. As the road curves right go over a stile on the left and up the steep slope towards a windbreak of trees. There are magnificent views back over Deanlane End and across the fields towards Stansted Forest and the outward leg of this walk.

Continue up through the trees to a stile beside a flint and brick cottage. Bear left along the crest of the hill. Pass through a gate and then cut across a windswept plateau, heading south towards Rowland's Castle. Eventually, you drop down the slope to a gate just before some houses. Follow a clear path alongside some barns and cottages. At a junction of tracks bear right and pass beside a thatched cottage. Continue for a few moments until the lane bends right by the entrance to The Barn, a private house.

Turn left at the footpath sign and walk down the drive and alongside the cottage to join a narrow path, with fields on the left and a wooden panel fence on the right. Pass between the gardens of some houses to reach the road. Cross over and go straight ahead between lines of houses and bungalows. This is Uplands Road. At the junction bear left and return to the centre of Rowland's Castle. At the T-junction turn right and return to the green where the walk began.

⑫ Buriton
The Master Robert

The Master Robert is situated on the edge of this pretty village, close to the South Downs. Originally several cottages, it has been extended and improved over the years and now offers an à la carte restaurant and hotel accommodation, as well as a snack menu and a cosy bar. The inn is named after the son of a previous owner. At one time it was known as the Maple.

For real ale drinkers there is a choice of Bass, Gale's HSB and Brakspear Bitter. There are also several guest ales. Guinness, Stella Artois and Labatts are available, and there is Scrumpy Jack for the cider drinker. As well as the bar and restaurant, there is a TV room where families or children on their own are welcome. The hotel's facilities include two conference rooms, one of which can adapt to a skittle alley. Outside is a large garden for the whole family to enjoy. Well-behaved dogs are welcome on a lead. The menu includes a selection of starters – soup of the day, the chef's own pâté and toast, and prawn cocktail, among them. Main courses range from the Master

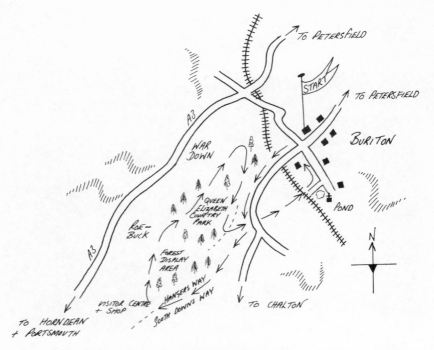

Robert Mixed Grill, breaded wholetail scampi and 6 oz sirloin steak to home-cooked carved ham, egg and chips and mushroom Stroganov. There are also salads, jacket potatoes, ploughman's, jumbos (a French stick and salad with various fillings) and a selection of sandwiches. There is a Sunday roast and a children's menu.

The times of opening are from 11.30 am to 3 pm and 6 pm to 11 pm on weekdays, 11 am to 3 pm and 6 pm to 11 pm on Saturdays, and 12 noon to 3 pm and 7 pm to 10.30 pm on Sundays.

Telephone: 0730 267275.

How to get there: Buriton is south of Petersfield, just off the A3. Follow the signs for the village and you will see the Master Robert as you enter Buriton.

Parking: You can park at the pub or in the vicinity of the church and village pond.

Length of the walk: 4 miles. Map: OS Landranger 197 Chichester and the Downs (inn GR 737203).

This is a stunning walk, offering glimpses of the South Downs – in particular Butser Hill – and joining forces with two long distance paths, the South Downs Way and the Hangers Way. Much of the route is within the Queen Elizabeth Country Park, an extremely popular amenity area. There is much to see and do within the glorious woodland.

The Walk

From the front of the Master Robert turn right and go straight over the crossroads into Kiln Lane towards Chalton. Walk up the lane away from the village. Go through the railway arch and then pass a signposted path on the right. Continue on up the hill, between banks of woodland, and at the top turn right at the entrance to Halls Hill car park. Swing immediately left to follow the route of two long distance footpaths – the South Downs Way and the Hangers Way. The latter route runs for 21 miles from Alton through the steep, wooded hillsides of Hampshire, via Selborne and Petersfield.

Cross a stile and walk ahead across the field. There are views of a cottage and some farm buildings over to your left. Pass through a wooden swing-gate and continue on the well-trodden path towards some woodland. Down below, in a fold in the hills, the road runs like a thread between steeply rising, grassy slopes. The scenery on this part of the walk is, without doubt, some of the finest anywhere in Hampshire. Go through another swing-gate and follow a woodland path until you reach a junction. Turn left and then right, descending the bank to reach a lower path.

Bear left and follow the clear track through the trees in a south-westerly direction. This is the edge of the Queen Elizabeth Country Park. Located at the western extremity of the South Downs, the 1,400 acre park offers a variety of recreational pursuits in a peaceful wooded setting. All around you are woodland trails, mountain bike trails and tracks for horse-riders and walkers. There are also guided walks, festivals and children's holiday activities.

Continue along the track, passing a barbecue area on the left, one of a number of such sites to be found within the boundaries

Buriton's pond and church.

of the park. Further on you reach an information point on the right of the track.

At the hairpin bend in the road bear right and follow it as it rises quite steeply between the trees. Soon it curves to the right. You are now on the western edge of the park. Traffic is visible down below, racing along the A3 in the distance. Head up the road, passing Windmill View. On the left, between the trees, are glimpses of distant downland. Butser Hill, marking the western boundary of the South Downs, is seen on this stage of the walk.

Follow the road up to the coach park and on the right is the Forest Display Area, where you can learn about the history and origins of trees in the vicinity. Continue on the main path, with the display area on the right. When you reach a sign for Roebuck, swing half-right to join a broad, grassy ride. Pass over the route of the mountain bike trail and continue through the trees. On the right are glimpses of the western half of the park, regimented lines of trees running to the distant horizon like a rumpled green carpet.

Eventually, you reach a wooden bench, beyond which is a junction. At this point bear right. As you do so, glance to the north for a spectacular view of rural Hampshire. Follow the path over War Down and descend between the trees. To the east is a magnificent view of the ridge of the South Downs in the distance. Pass a track running off sharp left and carry on a little further to the next junction. Bear sharp left here and walk along the track, with good views over this rolling countryside on the Hampshire/Sussex border. Drop down to the gate at Halls Hill car park. Walk down to the road, cross over and take the bridleway into the trees. Follow the path as it descends through the woodland, curves round to the right and passes through the railway arch. Continue beside the pretty gardens of a thatched cottage, Whistlers. Follow the lane as far as the village pond at Buriton. Walkers on the Hangers Way and the South Downs Way will be familiar with this landmark, a well-known feature on both routes.

Turn left and walk along the main street through Buriton, passing the village post office on the left and the Five Bells on the right. Continue to the next junction, where you will find the Master Robert on the right.

13 Droxford
The White Horse Inn

The precise age of this superb, rambling old coaching inn is not known but it has featured in many books and newspaper articles over the years. According to one source it is haunted by a friendly lady in grey. There is also a suggestion that it was a hostelry for fishermen on the nearby river Meon. Apparently you could learn to dance here at the turn of the century, though no one was allowed a partner unless they could do the steps solo. Inside the inn are lots of beams, low ceilings and a charming family room with comfy chairs, paintings and printed plates. There are lounge and public bars, a non-smoking restaurant, and overnight accommodation. The patio area outside is very popular on warmer days.

There is a good selection of real ales from the handpump, among them Wadworth 6X and Morland Old Speckled Hen. Autumn Gold and Dry Blackthorn draught ciders are available, as well as various bottled ciders. Guinness, Foster's and Kronenbourg are also on offer. The menu is impressive and includes a wide selection of dishes. There are starters, such as garlic bread and home-made soup, main dishes, ranging from vegetarian meals to home-made pie of the day, jumbo sausage or fish specialities, and a variety of snacks, for example, ploughman's, salads, sandwiches and hot crusty French sticks. There is a traditional Sunday roast and a 'Junior Menu'. Large groups should book and a menu will be sent.

The times of opening are 11 am to 3.30 pm and 6 pm to 11 pm between Monday and Saturday, and 12 noon to 3 pm and 7 pm to 10.30 pm on Sunday. The back bar is open all day on Saturday for drinks, rolls and sandwiches. It is requested that dogs are kept on a lead, preferably outside.

Telephone: 0489 877490.

How to get there: Droxford is on the A32 Fareham to Alton road. The inn is in the heart of the village, on the main road.

Parking: There is a car park at the back of the pub.

Length of the walk: 3½ miles. Map: OS Landranger 185 Winchester and Basingstoke (inn GR 606182).

The picturesque village of Droxford has close associations with the D-Day invasion of Europe. On a more peaceful note, it was also a favourite haunt of Izaak Walton. After a spell on high ground, with splendid views, the walk returns to Droxford through the delightful Meon valley.

The Walk
Emerging from the White Horse, turn right and walk down the village street as far as the entrance to the church of St Mary and All Saints. Droxford, with its elegant Georgian buildings, is one of the prettiest villages in the area. In 1944 it played a crucial part in the outcome of the Second World War. At the railway station, between the 2nd and 4th June, the War Cabinet and the Allied Chiefs stood poised to launch their invasion of Europe. Churchill and the other leaders, including Eisenhower, used this unlikely setting as the venue for their headquarters during that critical period, conducting operations in a special train based in a siding.

Pass through the wrought-iron gate into the churchyard,

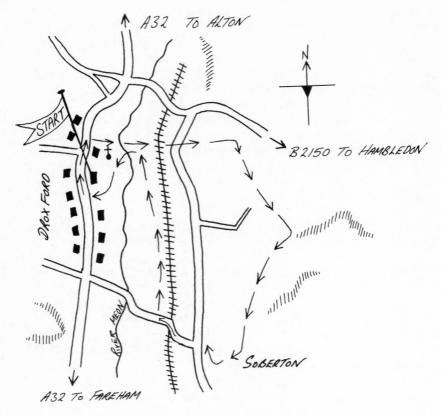

following the waymarkers for the Wayfarer's Walk. A plaque on the churchyard wall commemorates 'the men of the parish who died in the service of their country 1939-45'. The ten men who fell are individually named, along with their rank and the name of their regiment.

Follow the grassy path along the edge of the churchyard and, in the corner, swing right to join a paved section of path before veering left on to a wide, tree-lined path running down to the river Meon. Go through a gate and over a wooden footbridge with white railings. Izaak Walton fished here in the Meon, reflecting that the valley 'exceeds all England for swift, shallow, clear, pleasant brooks and store of trout.' His daughter married the local vicar.

Cross another footbridge and then leave the route of the Wayfarer's Walk, returning to it later on this walk. Make your way up the field to a gate in the top corner. From the gate there is a particularly memorable view of the valley and Droxford nestling on the west bank of the Meon. Go through the gate, disregarding one on the left, and head for several more gates in front of you, before joining a track which takes you over the old Meon Valley railway line. The line linked Alton with Fareham before it was discontinued some years ago. The former station building at Droxford is now a private house.

At the road bear left for several yards, then turn right, just beyond the entrance to Greylands. Follow the field boundary path and, at the hedge corner, swing right and walk along the clear downland path, defined by a distinctive turf strip, undulating through an expansive, windswept area of open farmland. Eventually, you come up the slope to meet a track. Turn right here and now the houses of Droxford and neighbouring Soberton can be seen straddling the valley floor. Follow the track as it curves right and then left. Head for a stile up ahead by a gate.

Cross the stile and walk ahead across another open field. Soon the path runs alongside a wire fence, beyond which sheep and spring lambs can sometimes be seen at the appropriate time of the year. Follow the boundary path down towards the road on the outskirts of Soberton. Cross the stile but don't actually join the road. Instead, take the track on the right just a couple of yards before it and follow it towards some corrugated barns. A parallel path on the left of the track takes you to the road in the centre of Soberton.

Turn right, pass the White Lion public house and then the turning to the church of St Peter. Immediately beyond it bear left (signposted 'Droxford and Swanmore'). Follow the road round to the right by Moor Hill and then left. Pass a large brick and flint house on the right. This is quite distinctive, with its turrets and crenellated design. Pass the route of the old Meon Valley line and then, just a little further down the lane, swing right to rejoin the Wayfarer's Walk.

This final stage of the walk is beside or near the Meon, cutting through fields and pretty meadows – a pleasing, pastoral landscape, highlighting some of Hampshire's gentlest and

Horses pause for refreshment in the Meon valley.

loveliest scenery. Follow the broad, grassy path along the valley floor. The disused railway embankment is visible through the trees on the right. Look for a stile up ahead and continue on the Wayfarer's Walk. The squat tower of Droxford church comes into view now, surrounded by trees.

Cross another stile and keep the hedgerow on your immediate left. At the next stile the Meon suddenly sweeps into view on the left. Follow the path, with the river now close by you. At the next stile turn left and retrace your steps back to the church at Droxford. Instead of turning right into the churchyard, go straight on along the left-hand side of the church and, when you draw level with it, follow the path as it bends left. Keep on the narrow path until you come to a stile in front of you and a track on the right.

Take the track and walk up to the main road. At this point there is a good view back over the Meon valley. Bear right at the road and very soon you reach the White Horse.

14 Owslebury
The Ship Inn

Located on a windswept chalk ridge, on the edge of the village, the Ship Inn has a strong nautical and sporting theme inside. The local cricket team is well illustrated in various photographs and there are lots of black and white prints of old ships decorating the walls. A slightly more unusual feature is the collection of bygone pub signs in the garden. Nostalgia lovers will also be drawn to the old advertisements for Grape Nuts and Sunlight Soap.

The Ship Inn is a well-known pub in the area and dates back 300 years. It is especially popular in summer. Inside, there is a quaint old bar with lots of character, low beams, log fires in winter and horse brasses. At the rear is a separate dining area, where families are welcome, and there are pleasant views overlooking the garden with its tables and benches and play area. There is a wide selection of bar meals from the specials board, as well as a good choice from the printed menu. Dishes include liver and sausage casserole, cottage pie and seafood

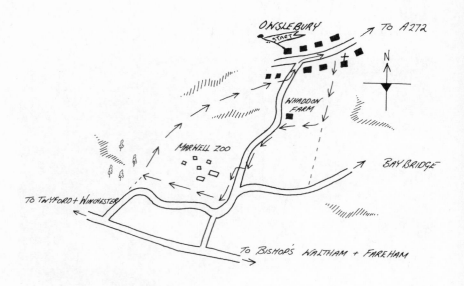

lasagne. There are also various burgers, home-made crêpes, steaks, ploughman's and jacket potatoes. A popular choice is 'The Ship Toastie' – two slices of French bread, ham, salami, mushroom, onion and peppers in melted cheese. Children's meals include chicken nuggets, jumbo sausage or fish fingers, all served with chips and baked beans. The selection of drinks includes Marston's Pedigree and Bitter, Banks's Mild from the handpump, McEwans, Stella Artois and Strongbow draught cider. Well-behaved dogs are welcome.

The times of opening are 11 am to 3 pm and 6 pm to 11 pm on Monday to Saturday and 12 noon to 3 pm and 7 pm to 10.30 pm on Sunday. Large groups are requested to book at weekends.

Telephone: 0962 777358.

How to get there: Owslebury is to the south-east of Winchester. From the city follow the B3335 to Twyford and then turn off for Morestead and Owslebury. The inn is west of the church in the village.

Parking: There is room to park at the inn.

Length of the walk: 3½ miles. Map: OS Landranger 185 Winchester and Basingstoke (inn GR 511233).

This is a bracing walk across open country, with glimpses of the world famous Marwell Zoological Park, an important wildlife centre for conservation and breeding. Much of the route is alongside Marwell's parkland and the return leg to Owslebury offers marvellous downland views.

The zoo is open to the public every day — between 10 am and 4 pm in winter and 10 am and 6 pm in summer. If you are planning a visit, it is advisable to allow most of the day, including the walk.

The Walk

Coming out of the inn, bear left towards Bramdean and Petersfield. Pass lines of brick and flint cottages and houses. Go on as far as The Old School House and then take the footpath to the right of the church, avoiding the waymarked path running through the churchyard. Walk parallel to its boundary wall and head down to the stile in the next fence. There are grand views to the south over the elevated, unpopulated downland country of mid-Hampshire.

After about 100 yards look for a wrought-iron gate on the right. Once through it, bear left and head down the slope to a stile which takes you into a paddock. Cross it to the next stile and then go straight ahead in the field beyond it to a bank and a line of trees. There is a stile hidden among them. Cross it and then turn right, heading towards the buildings of a smallholding. On reaching them, cross a ramshackle stile and briefly walk along a track to the road.

Turn left and head up the hill, following the country lane between hedgerows. At the top of the slope you will see a bridleway running parallel to the road, on the right. A sign advises riders that exotic animals and birds near the bridlepath may scare their horses. This is an obvious clue to the proximity of Marwell Zoo whose wire boundary fence is immediately beside the path. Follow the bridleway. Further on there are very good views of the splendid listed Tudor mansion and its 100 acres of parkland.

There are many children's amusements and attractions at Marwell, including a narrow gauge railway, running between the enclosures, and the 'encounter village' where visitors can

79

Tigers relaxing (courtesy of Marwell Zoo).

learn about the domestication of animals. Marwell places a strong emphasis on the value of education where wildlife is concerned.

Follow the path as it bends sharp right, away from the road. On the right are glimpses of more enclosures as well as the narrow gauge railway. The path runs along the edge of some trees and then plunges deep into the woodland. The buildings of Marwell Zoo remain visible on the right. Pass one of the entrances to the zoo and continue along the woodland track, sometimes saturated after rain. Eventually the path emerges from the trees and maintains the same direction across a patch of open ground, before entering another burst of woodland.

After a few yards you reach the main pedestrian entrance to Marwell and here you can deviate from the walk to visit the zoo and enjoy its many and varied attractions. After visiting Marwell Zoo return to the route and turn right at a waymarked bridleway to begin the next stage of the walk.

Follow the path along the edge of some woodland and pass over a track by a gate. A sign states that this is the 'Visitors' Car Park only. Horses prohibited'. Continue through the woods and soon you drop down a slope to a junction of paths. The bridleway continues straight ahead. However, the route of our walk is to the right at this point. Follow the waymarked path along the edge of some woodland, keeping the trees hard by you on the left. On the right you can spot the buildings and enclosures of Marwell. Look for a gap in the trees on the left and follow the path into the woodland. Bear right after several yards and continue in the same direction as before. Follow the clear path as it breaks from the trees. Herds of deer may sometimes be seen in the distance, on the grassy slopes to the north of the zoo complex. The open, downland scenery offered by this final leg of the walk is some of the best in this part of Hampshire. At length the path joins a concrete track running between houses and barn conversions. This is Orchard Court.

At the road turn left and return to the village centre in Owslebury. The Ship Inn is on the left as you come into the village.

15 Cheriton
The Flower Pots Inn

The Flower Pots is one of a dying breed of genuine, unpretentious village pubs where there is still a sense of the past. The inn lies in a side road, close to the village green at Cheriton. Either late Georgian or early Victorian, it was originally a farmhouse and even today it has the appearance of a family home – particularly the inviting, well-furnished family room with its choice of books and games. There are also quaint old lounge and public bars. At the time it was a farm, it was run for a while by a retired head gardener who gave it its present name.

The Flower Pots has the unusual distinction of being a pub with its very own brewery. The Cheriton Brewhouse was established in 1993 and provides reasonably priced real ale to many hostelries in the area. Naturally, the beer at the Flower Pots is all its own. The selection includes Pots Ale (light, dry and hoppy), Cheriton Best Bitter (copper, malty and hoppy) and Diggers Gold (golden, well-hopped bitter). There is also Carling

Black Label, Guinness and Bulmers Original cider. The pub grub is all home-cooked and includes soup, several ploughman's lunches, sweet and sour chicken, hot beef stew and chilli con carne. There is a choice of jacket potatoes and the inn is renowned for its toasties. Children's portions are available. The Flower Pots has a campsite and also offers overnight accommodation in an old converted barn, adjacent to the inn.

The times of opening are Monday to Saturday from 11.30 am to 2.30 pm and 6 pm to 11 pm. Sunday hours are 12 noon to 3 pm and 7 pm to 10.30 pm (no food on Sunday evening in winter).

Telephone: 0962 771318.

How to get there: Cheriton lies to the south of Alresford, on the B3046. Approaching from Alresford, turn right near the war memorial and the inn is on the left.

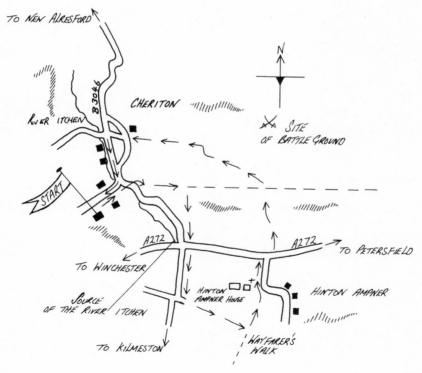

Parking: The Flower Pots has a car park. There is limited space elsewhere in Cheriton.

Length of the walk: 3¾ miles. Map: OS Landranger 185 Winchester and Basingstoke (inn GR 582283).

The walk passes close to the source of the Itchen and then heads for the 1,640-acre National Trust Hinton Ampner estate. The return leg to Cheriton is along the route of the Wayfarer's Walk, near the site of a Civil War battleground.

The Walk

Leave the pub by turning right and walking down to the junction in the centre of Cheriton. Bear right and walk along the B3046, passing the entrance to Cheriton House. Follow the road round a left bend and when it bends right, just before a thatched cottage, go straight on to join a track running beneath some yew trees. Follow the sunken track between hedgerows. Soon you reach a couple of bungalows and a greenhouse on the right. A few yards beyond the greenhouse is a junction of tracks. Turn right here and follow the sunken path down to merge with the road.

Go straight on and soon you reach a road junction by a red telephone box. Cross the A272 and take the road signposted 'Kilmeston' and 'Droxford'. Pass various houses and bungalows and then a burst of woodland on the left. As the road bends sharp right, bear left on to a muddy track running along the edge of the wood. Not far from this spot is the source of the Itchen, one of the great trout rivers of Hampshire.

Gradually the outline of Hinton Ampner House comes into view across the fields and parkland. The National Trust house and garden are open to the public during the summer months. 'Hinton' comes from the old English 'heatun', meaning 'village on high ground' while the 'Ampner' in the name is derived from 'almoner'.

The neo-Georgian house was expertly rebuilt and restored as recently as the 1960s, following a fire which almost completely destroyed a fine collection of furniture and paintings belonging to the then owner, Ralph Dutton, the 8th Lord Sherborne. Dutton was returning to the house from the nearby woods one

84

The village of Cheriton.

day in 1960 when he spotted smoke billowing from the building. Hinton Ampner stands on the site of several houses, dating back to 1550, that were either demolished or destroyed by fire. Many different and unusual species of trees were planted around the house and village, including Spanish chestnut, Turkey oak and Norway maple, to provide peaceful walks and pleasing vistas.

Continue across this stretch of fine Hampshire countryside and soon you come to the route of the Wayfarer's Walk at the point where it crosses our path. The Wayfarer's Walk is one of many long distance routes devised by Hampshire County Council and intended to take advantage of the county's varied range of scenery. The way runs for 70 miles between Inkpen Beacon in Berkshire to the south coast at Emsworth.

Turn left, noting the arrows indicating the route of the Wayfarer's Walk, and follow the path through a gate and along the left-hand boundary of the field, keeping the elegant frontage of Hinton Ampner House in view between the trees. Cross the parkland – with the hedge and fence on your left – and look for a white gate on the left, and nearby cottage. Make for the gate and, with Hinton Ampner's Saxon church in front of you, turn right and pass through some wrought iron gates. Walk down the drive, passing between lines of yew trees. Just before the road junction there is a telegraph pole by an old red telephone box. Look for the sign attached to the pole, 'telegrams may be telephoned', a reminder of the early days of telecommunication.

At the junction, by Yew Tree Cottage, go straight over the main road and continue along the Wayfarer's Walk (signposted 'Inkpen Beacon 42 miles'). Follow the track between hedgerows, with a red-brick cottage on the right. Begin a gentle ascent at this stage of the route.

The views over wide, spacious landscapes are impressive. With a strong imagination it is possible to see how this tract of countryside might have looked in the spring of 1644, when it was the scene of an important Civil War battle between the Parliamentarians, led by Sir William Waller, and the Royalist Army, under Sir Ralph Hopton. It became a Parliamentary victory which halted the Royalist advance towards London. However, the death toll was high, with as many as 2,000 slain. According to popular legend, the blood of the dead and the injured flowed like a river through the surrounding country lanes – a common description applied to many bloody Civil War confrontations. The mounds in this area are reputed to mark the graves of soldiers who took part in the battle.

At a junction of tracks go forward for a couple of yards and then take the path running up the left-hand bank. Cross the stile and then head diagonally across the field to the far right corner. This is a windswept part of the walk, the breeze whipping across the open downland. There are good views over to the parkland at Hinton Ampner. Exit from the field, turn right and then immediately left, over a stile. Continue on the route of the Wayfarer's Walk, crossing the field and going over the stile and into the next field. Follow the field edge and, in the corner, join a narrow path between fences and hedgerows.

Further down, the path runs between wooden panel fences. At the end of the path, back in the village of Cheriton, bear right towards the bridge over the Itchen. Cross over, still on the Wayfarer's Walk, and then bear left by the white bridge. Veer left again, almost immediately, and at the road turn left and walk along towards the war memorial. On the right is a private house with the letters 'HH' on its front elevation. The house used to be an inn, named after the Hampshire Hunt. On the left is the pretty village green, overlooked by a variety of picturesque houses and cottages. Cheriton has been the proud recipient of the Best Kept Village award on several occasions.

Turn right, just beyond the war memorial, and return to the inn.

16 Itchen Abbas
The Trout Inn

The Trout lies in the lovely Itchen valley. The rural surroundings have changed little since the summer of 1862, when Charles Kingsley stayed here and wrote part of the children's classic *The Water Babies*. In those days the inn was known as the Plough. In a letter, Kingsley wrote, 'Oh, the loveliness of this vale and river! It is a happy land round here. I am just starting fishing – day looking perfect: but I don't hope for much, the fish are all feeding at ground . . . I have had bad sport enough; so has everyone – but delightful scenery. I am now at the Plough at Itchen.' The river here almost certainly inspired Kingsley to write about the underwater exploits of Tom, the little chimney sweep.

The Trout is a perfect venue for a drink and something to eat after a walk beside the Itchen. It is a pub of great character and caters for both adults and children. Well-behaved dogs on a lead are also welcome. Marston's Pedigree and Bitter are among the real ales and Foster's, Heineken, Stella Artois and Swan Light are also served. Strongbow draught cider is available too. The Trout is renowned for traditional British cooking and local trout is a speciality. There is also a choice of steak and kidney pudding, liver and bacon, roast chicken, battered jumbo cod and gammon steak. The snacks include soup, a selection of freshly made sandwiches, a range of toasted open sandwiches and there is a specials board as well. Children's meals are also available – including fish fingers and burgers – and family meals can be enjoyed in the special dining area. Outside there is a garden and play area.

The times of opening are Monday to Saturday from 11 am to 3 pm and 6 pm to 11 pm, and on Sunday from 12 noon to 3 pm and 7 pm to 10.30 pm.

Telephone: 0962 779537.

How to get there: Itchen Abbas is on the B3047 between Winchester and Alresford. The inn is on the main road.

Parking: The car park at the back of the inn is the most suitable place to leave a car whilst undertaking this walk.

Length of the walk: 3 miles. Map: OS Landranger 185 Winchester and Basingstoke (inn GR 536328).

The gentle waters of the Itchen provide a constant source of delight on this charming walk. There is also a Georgian church to see, and, at Avington Park, an amenity area where you can relax in pleasant rural surroundings and enjoy views of the lake. On the final leg of the walk is the site of the country home of Viscount Gray, Secretary of State during the First World War.

The Walk
From the inn go straight across the road and take the turning to Avington. Note the church of St John the Baptist on the right. The lychgate has an inscription which reads, 'Set up in grateful memory of our parents Henry Thomas Gillson and Anne Ellen his wife, 1933, RIP'. Adjacent to the lychgate is a cross dedicated to 'Christopher Byron Simpson, Captain in the Royal Fusiliers, who fell on the field of honour in France in the Great European War, October 7th 1916, aged 22'. The cross is also in remembrance of those others who made the great sacrifice.

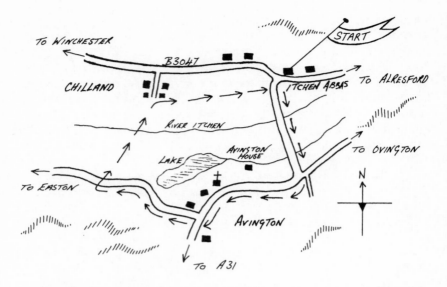

Continue along the road and soon you cross the river Itchen at a glorious spot. The river divides into various streams and tributaries in this part of the Itchen valley. Follow the road through an avenue of yew trees – so common to this part of Hampshire – and shortly you come to a pretty weir, delightfully situated in the shade of the trees. Just beyond the road bridge is one of the imposing entrances to Avington Park on the right.

Follow the road round to the right and at this stage of the walk there are constant glimpses of Avington Park through the trees. The splendid porticoed house is 18th century and once belonged to John Shelley, brother of the poet. Charles II also stayed here with Nell Gwynn. There are pretty views over the Itchen valley – a combination of meadows, undulating fields and distant woodland. This is Hampshire river valley scenery at its best.

Pass various houses and cottages and an old pre-Telecom red telephone box. On the right is the entrance to St Mary's, an unspoilt Georgian church and one of the most perfect in the country. It dates from about 1770. Unfortunately, funds are urgently needed to protect and preserve this historic building.

Follow the road as it bears left by a letter-box and now you will see the remains of the old village well, further up near a row of brick and flint cottages. Look for a turning on the right to Easton and Winchester. Note the old-fashioned signpost here – black writing on a white background. During the Second World War these signs were constantly uprooted or moved, in order to confuse the enemy in the event of England being invaded.

Pass a footpath on the left which runs along the edge of a field fringed by woodland. Soon you are treated to a splendid sight. Ahead of you is the entrance to Avington Park, an amenity area in the care of Hampshire County Council. From the grassy slopes there is a magnificent view across a lake to the main house seen earlier in the walk. The smooth expanse of water adds a classic touch to this memorable scene. The lake stretches into the distance and the white flecks on its serene surface are swans gliding in the water. An ideal spot for a picnic.

Continue along the road and, up ahead, a cedar tree stands out in a windbreak. Follow the road into some woodland and soon you pass a pretty cottage with a slate roof and an ornate portico. Trees and the winding, lazy streams of the Itchen can be seen beside the road. When the road emerges from the cover

A view of Avington Park and its lake.

of the trees, look for a wooden footbridge on the right. Cross it and follow a wide path through a landscape of marshes and reed beds in this low-lying part of Hampshire.

Cross several footbridges and the Itchen on a pretty stretch of the river, then pass the entrance to Chilland Ford, a house. All around you are attractive houses and cottages set in their own spacious grounds. Bear right at a sign, 'Drive slowly, children and dogs', and join a path between fences and brick walls. This is the Itchen Way.

Soon the path runs alongside the Itchen, providing exceptionally striking views of the river and its peaceful valley setting. In spring a profusion of daffodils adds a splash of colour. The path can get muddy here, after rain, but it soon becomes grassy at the point where it ascends gently to the higher ground. Go through a kissing gate and follow the line of the fence. There are houses and gardens on your immediate left. Just before the next gate is a small enclosed copse over in the corner of the field. According to the plaque beside the fence, it is the 'Site of the Hampshire Cottage – Edward, Viscount Gray of Fallodon – Wykehamist, author, statesman, 1862 – 1933, and his wife Dorothy. It was to us a lovely refuge.' Viscount Gray and his wife used the cottage to escape the pressures of political life. Sadly, it burned to the ground in the 1920s.

Go through the gate in the field corner, cross over a track lined by trees and continue on the Itchen Way. The river is still visible on the right. Avington Park can also be seen, amid the trees. Go through a latched gate and down to the road. Bear left to the junction and return to the inn.

Lower Wield

17 Lower Wield
The Yew Tree

Built as a private house about 300 years ago, this attractive inn, standing in the shadow of an old yew tree, has been a public house since the turn of the century. The cosy interior includes exposed brick walls, low beams and horse brasses. Look out for the aerial photograph of the pub and a painting entitled 'The Scratching Beagle' – dogs playing bar billiards!

There are several bars and a large dining area, where families are welcome. The Yew Tree is a 'foody' country pub, with a varied menu that changes daily. Fresh fish from Cornwall is one of its specialities. There is a choice of starters or light meals, and the main courses include steak and kidney pie, pan-fried river trout, grilled rump steak and grilled fillet steak, with a traditional roast on Sundays. Also on offer is a range of jacket potatoes, ploughman's and baguettes. Sandwiches are made to order. The Yew Tree offers a variety of desserts as well, including individually baked bread and butter pudding and a selection of ice-creams. A blackboard menu lists further choices and children's portions are also available. Real ales at this popular pub come from the Cheriton Brewhouse and include Pots Ale and Diggers Gold. For the lager drinker there is Stella Artois and Foster's, while for the cider enthusiast there is Strongbow. The Yew Tree has a pleasant beer garden and children's play area, with views over open fields. Dogs are welcome, but only in the garden, please. The village cricket ground is opposite the pub, players and supporters tending to adjourn to the Yew Tree after a match.

The times of opening are weekdays from 12 noon to 3 pm and 6 pm to 11 pm (closed on Monday evenings), and Sundays from 12 noon to 3 pm and 7 pm to 10.30 pm (no food on Sunday evenings). It is advisable to book for Sunday lunch and on bank holidays. Larger groups are asked to make a reservation.

Telephone: 0256 389224.

How to get there: From Basingstoke take the A339 Alton road, then join the B3046 Alresford road. At Preston Candover turn left for Lower Wield. Follow the signs for the village and the inn is on the left.

Parking: There is room to park at the Yew Tree.

Length of the walk: 2¾ miles. Map: OS Landranger 185 Winchester and Basingstoke (inn GR 636397).

This is a peaceful country walk, crossing the open farmland of the Candover valley. The return leg is along a tree-lined track, with pleasant views over fields and woods.

The Walk

Emerge from the inn and turn right. Walk up the lane between banks and hedgerows, passing thatched Hut Cottage. By the gate for Dials Close take the right-hand footpath. Go over a stile and across the field. There are striking views either side of the path. On the left are glimpses of the open pastoral country around the charming village of Preston Candover. To the right the view is of rolling farmland, interspersed with woodland and hedgerows. Cross the next stile and go out to the road.

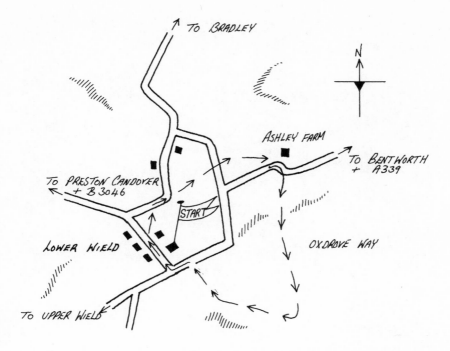

Bear right and follow a pretty, tree-lined lane. On the right is a section of white fencing by the entrance to Kings Farm. In spring and early summer yellow daisies and clusters of daffodils grow in colourful profusion. When the road bends sharp left, swing right on to a muddy track. Turn left immediately and follow the field boundary, keeping the hedge hard by you on the left. Cross another stile and continue, with uninterrupted views over open countryside.

In the field corner go out to the lane, cross over and continue along the edge of the next field. Go through the gap in the hedge into the next field. The route of this walk is now diagonally right as the path heads across the field, passing a lightly wooded hollow. Keep the hollow on the left and make for a gap in the southern boundary of the field. Pass through the hedge and cross the next field, by veering slightly left almost to its bottom left-hand corner.

Go through another gap and out to the road. Turn left and walk along the lane towards Ashley Farm. A small duck-pond

95

A solitary duck at Ashley Farm.

can be seen on the left as the lane curves round to the right beside the entrance to the farm. After only a few yards the road bears left. At this point you leave it by joining a muddy track – the OS Pathfinder map refers to this section of the walk as 'Dirty Track'! This is the route of the Oxdrove Way, a cross-country route, probably used in Saxon times for driving sheep and cattle. The track cuts through the Hampshire countryside and here the scene is a timeless rural picture of fields, hedgerows and pretty copses.

After about ¾ mile you come to a junction of tracks. Turn right here and leave the route of the Oxdrove Way, following a stony track through the trees. After a few yards it becomes quite muddy and rutted underfoot. Ignore a track running off into the trees on the left and follow the main path as it veers right and up the slope. Continue for over ½ mile along this rough track. On a summer's day,the overhanging trees provide shelter from the sun. Between the branches there are glimpses of surrounding fields. Eventually, you reach the road.

Bear left and then almost immediately right (signposted 'Lower Wield'). Walk along the lane and back to the inn.

18 Rowledge
The Hare and Hounds

The Hare and Hounds lies on the Hampshire/Surrey border, in the centre of this pleasant, sprawling village. Alice Holt Forest is just a few hundred yards away. The inn is thought to be late Georgian or early Victorian and is understood to have been built as a brewery, possibly part of the old Farnham United Brewery. Inside, there is the main bar, an attractive restaurant overlooking the garden and two adjacent small dining-rooms, which are among the inn's most popular features. Families are welcome and the garden is an outstanding attraction for both children and adults. There is a play area with swings and, elsewhere, many bushes, shrubs and flower borders. Those who enjoy gardening will surely be impressed. The summertime barbecue is very popular here. Dogs are welcome, but only in the garden.

The Hare and Hounds specialises in home-made food and included in the traditional bar fare are various ploughman's lunches and sandwiches. For something a little more

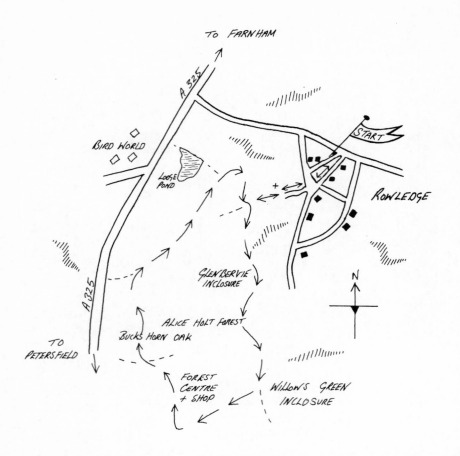

substantial, you could choose steak and kidney pie, scampi, bangers and mash, 8 oz sirloin steak, gammon steak or omelette, among a range of dishes. There are children's portions, a traditional roast on Sunday and an à la carte menu. The cask ales include Morland Bitter, Old Masters and Original Best Bitter. There is also draught Bombardier, Stella Artois, Foster's and Guinness. Gaymers Olde English cider is available, too.

The times of opening are from 11.30 am to 3 pm and 6 pm to 11 pm, open all day on summer Saturdays. On Sundays the hours are 12 noon to 3 pm and 7 pm to 10.30 pm. Larger groups are asked to book, particularly for the restaurant.

Telephone: 0252 792287.

How to get there: Rowledge is on the Surrey border, south of Farnham. It is easily reached from the A325 (Petersfield to Farnham Road), north of Bordon Camp. Follow Fullers Road (signposted 'Rowledge') and the inn will be found on the right in the village square.

Parking: There is room to park at the inn and in the village.

Length of the walk: 4 miles. Map: OS Landranger 186 Aldershot and Guildford (inn GR 823433).

The walk begins on the county boundary with Surrey and then quickly makes for the peace and tranquility of Alice Holt Forest. Apart from a few hundred yards at the start and finish, the entire walk is within the boundaries of this ancient, beautiful woodland. Halfway round the route is a visitor centre and shop where refreshments are available.

The Walk

From the front of the Hare and Hounds go forward for a few yards and then bear right into Cherry Tree Road. Detached houses and pleasant spacious gardens line the road. Pass the Cherry Tree Inn on the right and at the war memorial go straight on into Church Lane. When the road bends right towards the parish church of St James, continue ahead on a waymarked path into Alice Holt Forest. There are plantations and areas of established woodland either side of the clear, well-used path.

After several hundred yards you come to a major junction of tracks. Avoid the first turning on the left, instead taking the second one on the left. This is the route of the popular cycle trail, as denoted by a series of wooden posts carrying a bicycle symbol. Very soon the track begins to drop down steadily between lines of trees. At the bottom of the slope pass over another junction of tracks and continue on the cycle trail.

Soon the track descends once more between the trees, before ascending the next hillside. Cross another junction of tracks and soon you are climbing quite steeply through the forest. There is always much to see in the woodland. Norway spruce and Corsican pine are among the most common species of tree on this particular route. The largest animals to be found within the forest are deer, whose presence here dates back to the time

Alice Holt was part of a royal hunting ground. There are several badger sets within the forest, but these fascinating, reclusive animals are hard to spot. The sound of birdsong is one of the great pleasures of a stroll in Alice Holt Forest. Between April and July the distinct songs of warblers can be heard, especially willow warblers, garden warblers and chiff-chaffs. Many other examples of birdlife can be seen in the area – as well as a rich variety of flora, including herbs and grasses, sedges and rushes. Butterflies are particularly prolific – there are nearly 30 different species, among them the white admiral and the purple emperor.

Continue up the slope and on the left, beyond the clearings and the open ground, there are glimpses of distant wooded horizons. Follow the cycle track as it undulates through the forest. The track runs down between lines of pine and spruce and here the soothing sound of the breeze in the branches adds to the enjoyment of the walk. Follow the track as it loops round to the right and here there is a turning on the left on the edge of a forest clearing.

Keep to the main cycle track and follow it into thick woodland. When you reach a fork veer right, looking for the cycle trail symbols. Climb gently through the trees and further up you can see the forest visitor centre and parking area, over to the right among the trees. Woodland vistas over distant afforested slopes during this walk illustrate the sheer size and scale of Alice Holt Forest and its neighbouring woodland – surprising when you consider the close proximity of towns such as Farnham, Aldershot, Bracknell and Guildford.

Follow the trail until you are about 50 yards from the road and a gate. At this point turn right and follow a clear, stony path between young trees and banks of bracken. Make for the car park and the visitor centre and shop beyond. More information about Alice Holt Forest is available here, and refreshment can also be obtained at the site.

As you approach the building the cycle trail veers off to the left of it. Keep following it, looking for the colour-coded posts and symbols. Follow the track down the slope and then bear sharp right at the bottom. This part of the forest is known as Bucks Horn Oak. Not far away to the left is the A325. The cycle trail sweeps round to the right. Continue on the wide track,

Lodge Pond.

crossing over a junction of paths. Pass a barrier and keep following the track. Further on, look for a junction where there is a path on the left and two paths on the right, one of them shooting off half-right. Take the path running off to the left of the cycle trail and follow it down to the banks of Lodge Pond. This is a popular feature of Alice Holt Forest, the pond prettily fringed by woodland.

If you wish, you can extend the walk to nearby Birdworld at this point, though this involves a short stretch on the main road. Return to the pond and retrace your steps to the cycle trail, bearing left when you reach it.

Follow the track as it curves round to the right. At the next junction turn left and follow the path back to the Hare and Hounds at Rowledge, via the parish church, war memorial and Cherry Tree Road.

19 Crookham Village
The Chequers

The Chequers is a popular inn, conveniently close to the restored Basingstoke Canal. Walkers, fishermen, canal enthusiasts and holidaymakers boating on the canal all find their way here for a leisurely pint and perhaps something to eat. The inn was run by members of the same family for 300 years before closing in the 1980s. After extensive restoration it reopened in 1991, with a spacious interior, consisting of a single bar, an eating area and a sunny conservatory. In the heyday of the canal era the Chequers was a favourite haunt of canal workers and bargees, as were many pubs on this and other canals. There is also a suggestion that it might be haunted. According to some sources, a wall at the inn often assumes a reddish look – giving the impression that it is soaked with blood. However, the landlord claims the only spirits he has seen are the ones he sells his customers!

Several real ales are on offer, including Badgers Best and Tanglefoot, with Dry Blackthorn for the cider drinker and

Kronenbourg and Pilsner for the lager enthusiast. There is a specials board, and an extensive menu which consists of various starters – smoked salmon platter, hot curried prawns and deep-fried potato skins, among them – while main courses include home-made steak and kidney pie, traditional sausages and mash, lasagne verdi and whole rainbow trout. There are omelettes and various dishes from the grill, salads and vegetarian meals. Ploughman's, sandwiches and a children's menu are also available, as is a range of sweets. A traditional roast is served on Sunday. Dogs are welcome in the vicinity of the bar, but away from the eating area and conservatory. Outside is a pleasant beer garden and children's play area.

The times of opening are Monday to Friday from 11 am to 3 pm and 5.30 pm to 11 pm, and all day on Saturday (11 am to 11 pm). The Sunday hours are 12 noon to 3 pm and 7 pm to 10.30 pm. Booking can be a good idea.

Telephone: 0252 615336.

How to get there: Crookham village lies north-west of Aldershot and between the M3 and the A287. If using the motorway leave at junction 5 and at Odiham follow the A287 east towards

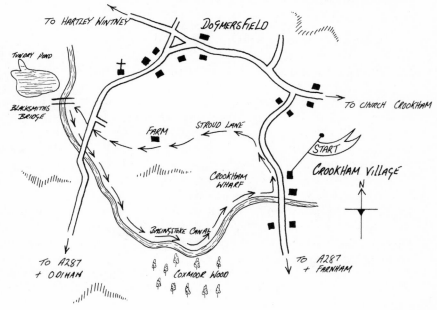

A narrowboat on the Basingstoke Canal.

Farnham. The turning to Crookham Village is on the left and is signposted. Go over the canal bridge and the inn is on the right after a short distance.

Parking: There is a spacious car park at the pub. Alternatively, you could park at nearby Chequers Bridge.

Length of the walk: 3 miles. Map: OS Landranger 186 Aldershot and Guildford (inn GR 793518).

Crookham Village lies on the north bank of the Basingstoke Canal. The first half of this easy circuit is along field paths and tracks, with delightful views over unspoilt tracts of countryside – a striking mixture of trees and open farmland. The return leg is along the towpath of the retored Basingstoke Canal, cutting through bursts of pretty, peaceful woodland. On this stretch you may find yourself in conversation with the occupants of passing canal boats – their speed unlikely to exceed yours!

The Walk

From the car park turn right and walk along the road beside a line of private houses. When you reach a bridge over the river Hart, bear left into Stroud Lane. The pretty, timber-framed cottage on the left – Strangers Corner – is reputedly haunted. Follow the track between the trees and soon it reaches the entrance to Willow Cottage. Veer to the left of the cottage, on a grassy path.

After only a few yards you will see a stile in the left-hand boundary. Cross it and follow the direction of the yellow waymarker arrow to the next stile in the right-hand boundary of the field. Once over it, walk straight ahead on a clear field path, with an area of pretty woodland on the right. Pass under some pylons and begin a gentle ascent to the top of a slope. Drop down the other side and make for a gap in the trees ahead.

Pass a footpath sign and follow the track through the woodland. At this point the walk crosses several tributary streams stemming from the river Hart, one of Hampshire's lesser-known rivers. Follow the track round to the right, to cut between several isolated houses. Go up the track between hedges and trees. After only a matter of yards you will see a stile in the left bank. Take the stile into the paddock and head diagonally right towards a stile located among some conifer trees.

Cross over two more stiles in quick succession and then follow a narrow path between wire fences. After about 75 yards it bears sharp right to terminate at another stile. There are expansive views from this stretch of the walk, over a gently swelling landscape of woods and fields.

Follow the clear path diagonally across the field. The road and various houses and cottages are visible in the distance. To the right you can see the buildings of Dogmersfield. The path curves right beneath some power cables and runs straight to the road. Cross it and join a narrow path cutting between houses. Moments later the walk joins a track running along the edge of some dense woodland. Soon it curves to the left and goes up to Blacksmiths Bridge.

From the bridge there are glimpses of nearby Tundry Pond. The pond covers about 20 acres and occupies a pleasant parkland setting. Originally, it was part of Dogmersfield Park.

The main house, a large Georgian mansion, is about a ½ mile from the route of this walk. Henry VI often stayed at Dogmersfield and, in the 19th century, it was the home of Sir Henry Mildmay, who carried out sweeping changes during his time there. He enlarged the house and the pond, redesigned the parkland, moved the village further away, because he felt it was too close, and refused permission for the Basingstoke Canal to cross his land. By looking at the route of the canal on the OS map, you can see that his refusal resulted in the Basingstoke Canal Company devising an expensive and circuitous alternative route along the northern boundary of the estate.

Blacksmiths Bridge was built in 1792 and restored in 1976. It is one of a number of such bridges on the 37 miles of the Basingstoke Canal. The canal was completed in 1794 and was originally intended to be a major commercial route between London and North Hampshire. However, the canal never fulfilled its early promise and eventually it fell into decline. The dawning of the railway era also furthered its downfall. Thanks to extensive and dedicated restoration in recent years, the canal is now run as a linear leisure park. Boat trips are available and you can hire rowing boats or launch your own craft.

The return leg of the walk is now along the eastbound towpath of the canal. Walk along it, with the waterway on your immediate right. Cruising narrow boats may be seen along this stretch, lending a touch of colour to the walk. Pass under the road bridge and beside a huge overhanging oak tree. On the opposite bank is an unusual Dutch-style house, set in its own spacious grounds. Beyond it is a picturesque, timber-framed house. In spring its colourful garden is a thick carpet of daffodils.

The canal meanders between bursts of light woodland and at various intervals there are glimpses of distant countryside. Pass an old wartime pill-box and now the woodland becomes thicker either side of the canal, with much to interest the walker and naturalist all around. There are lines of oak and silver birch trees, among many other species, and the pretty woods often echo to the delightful sound of birdsong. Here the Basingstoke Canal is a quiet and peaceful rustic haven.

Further on, there are the remains of an old bridge across the canal. Continue on the towpath and soon the trees thin to reveal glimpses of farmland. Pass between further lines of trees, to reach the old wharf at Crookham Village. There is a picnic and parking area just beside Chequers Bridge. At this point you can read in detail about the history of the canal and the hard work that has led to its restoration. Bear left at the road and return to the inn, which will be found after a couple of hundred yards.

20 Mattingley
The Leather Bottle

The Leather Bottle dates back to 1714 and was built as an inn. Originally, it was partly a pub and partly a cottage and, in those days, it was known as the White Lion. Inside, there are oak beams and wintertime log fires, among other traditional features. The Leather Bottle is popular in the area and often becomes very busy. The clientele is a mixture of passing trade and locals. Apart from the bar there is the cottage room, where families are welcome. There is also a spacious garden at the side, with tables and benches and a children's area.

Among the real ales are Directors and Courage Best, served from casks behind the bar. A guest beer, which is often a strong ale, is also on offer. Draught cider includes Dry Blackthorn. Food is served every day. Starters range from prawn cocktail, pâté and toast to breaded mushrooms and soup. There are ploughman's lunches and suppers, a selection of traditional dishes, including chilli con carne, lasagne, salads, chicken Kiev and steak. There is a specials board and lighter snacks include sirloin steak sandwich, prawn sandwich and jacket potato. 'Tom's Special' – a toasted sandwich with ham and mushrooms inside and a fried egg sunnyside up on top – is, according to the menu, named after the intelligent chap who ordered this delight every day!

The times of opening are Monday to Saturday from 11 am to 2.30 pm and 6 pm to 11 pm, and on Sunday from 12 noon to 2.30 pm and 7 pm to 10.30 pm. Larger parties and groups are asked to ring in advance. No dogs, please.

Telephone: 0734 326371.

How to get there: Mattingley is on the B3349 between junction 11 of the M4 and junction 5 of the M3. The inn is at the southern end of the village.

Parking: There is plenty of room to park at the inn. It is not advisable to park elsewhere as the B3349 is a busy road.

Length of the walk: 4 miles. Map: OS Landranger 186 Aldershot and Guildford (inn GR 733575).

This is a delightful walk of immense variety in the pretty, pastoral valley of the river Whitewater. There are no steep hills, only a couple of short, gentle ascents. The main highlights include several stretches of the Whitewater and views of West Green House – an early 18th century house, of imposing design, in the care of the National Trust. Eventually, the path reaches Mattingley church. Originally it was a barn but it was converted about 600 years ago to a chapel-of-ease. This explains the timber-framed construction, infilled with herringbone brickwork. The design is most unusual and certainly very striking.

The Walk

From the inn turn left and walk along the road for a short distance until you reach a right-hand curve and a sign for Bartletts Farm. Bear left at this point and go over the stile. Soon you begin to approach the farm buildings. Go through some double gates before you reach them and then bear left for several yards to a stile. Join a broad, grassy path, with the farm buildings on your right.

Head down into the dip. The view ahead is of a pleasant

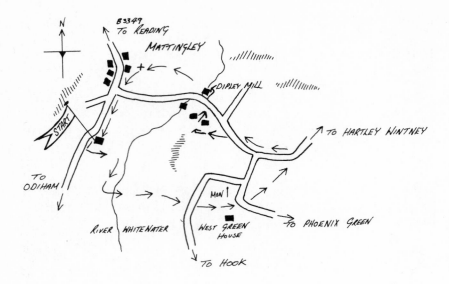

patchwork of fields and woodland. Pass between some trees to arrive at a field edge. Turn right, walk along the field boundary and soon you will see a footbridge in the field corner. The direction of the path is very clear here, a series of signs and waymarkers indicating the route of the walk. Cross the river Whitewater and follow the clear path to the top right-hand corner of the field. There is woodland on your right.

Cross a stream to a track and bear left. After about 80 yards follow the track round to the right. Continue along the field edge, with a hedge on the immediate right. Behind you are pretty views over the valley. At the top of the slope bear left and walk alongside a timber shooting hut. Swing right and go up the clear track between trees and hedgerows. Pass a bungalow on the left, Damales, and, at the road, turn right for a few yards.

Go through an impressive wrought-iron gate on the left and follow the waymarked path across the parkland of West Green House. There is a line of trees over to the right. In the distance is a curious, 50 ft high column bearing a Latin inscription. The English translation is as follows, 'this monument was built with a great deal of money which otherwise some day would have been given into the hands of the public revenue 1976, Robert Alistair McAlpine'.

Mattingley's timber framed church.

Aim for another set of wrought iron gates in the far boundary and go out to the road. Look out for a good view of West Green House as you approach the gates. The entrance to the house is on the right. Opposite the gates join a splendid avenue of oak trees, one of the highlights of this varied walk. The oaks were planted by Lady Mildmay, one time lady of the manor at West Green. William Cobbett, renowned for his *Rural Rides*, viewed them with approval when he visited this part of Hampshire in 1821.

The woodland ride is used by walkers and riders. On the left the tall McAlpine monument can be glimpsed between the trees. Glancing back, there is a striking view of West Green House, framed by the trees. Follow the avenue of oaks to the road and then turn left by the Dutch House. Follow the broad verge and here you will see the results of extensive coppicing, part of a long-term management plan prepared by the Hampshire Wildlife Trust in conjunction with local councils and the Forestry Commission, with the aim of improving the quality of the woodland.

Pass a turning on the left and continue towards Dipley. A red telephone box is visible on the left. Soon you reach a footpath on the left between two bungalows, Cotswold and White Knights. Take the path and follow it as it runs across open fields, passing beneath some power cables. Descend a gentle slope to some trees and a stile. Join a narrow path along the edge of some woodland and then follow a drive running between various houses, cottages and bungalows. Following the drive round to the right, pass through more woodland and then alongside more cottages and modern, executive-style houses. At the road bear left for several yards and then right to a stile. Follow a grassy path along the field edge for several hundred yards and then turn left and cross the field on another waymarked path. Cross a stile, then the river Whitewater near Dipley Mill. The surroundings at this stage of the walk are particularly pleasant, the river flowing through a stretch of pretty, peaceful countryside.

Turn right and follow the riverbank. Cross another stile, go under some power lines and then look for a waymarker arrow. Swing left at this point, away from the water and make for a gate in the field boundary. Join a muddy track and follow it up the slope. Pass through some gates at the top and then bear right. As you approach some farm buildings the outline of Mattingley church becomes apparent. Take the stile into the churchyard and pass to the right of this distinctive, timber-framed place of worship. At the main gate bear left by a black and white timber-framed cottage and follow a waymarked path into the woodland. Fir trees, holly trees and banks of undergrowth line your route. Pass alongside a wall, cross a drive and continue on the path. Soon you join a drive leading to the road. Walk alongside the verge of the main B3349 road for several hundred yards, back to the inn.